PEEKS at the PAST

in Sheffield and the surrounding area
By Ann Beedham

Volume 2

Detail of the Wirksworth Slab

Copyright Pickard Communication, 10-11 Riverside Park, Sheaf Gardens, Sheffield S2 4BB
Telephone 0114 2757222 or 2757444 Facsimile 0114 2758866 email info@picomm.co.uk
Illustrations, graphics and photographs by Ann Beedham unless otherwise stated

Contents

This book is another small peek at the past - a look at features, places and people from earlier days, that are standing parallel with or connected to our everyday surroundings in some way. Whether it be old mill wheel that remains hidden in grass at the feet of modern day ramblers, or an old building with a new use hidden amongst the traffic and office blocks, these past traces are part of the continuing stream of life in Sheffield and surrounds.

The cobbles of earlier streets peek through the asphalt, carvings from hands long dead gaze on scenes their creators never dreamed of and old buildings welcome new generations of visitors through their well tread doorways.

As before, these pages are not meant to be a scholarly text or detailed history, but to point to some of the wonderful and most fascinating artwork, lifestories and places we

have around us.

Whilst working on this book I have again met many enthusiastic and helpful people only too happy to share their memories and knowledge, as well as their time. That has been part of the pleasure, as well as finding out new things and exploring new places.

I hope you find something of interest to explore yourself, or to set you gazing anew at places you are familiar with.

I have tried to check any facts mentioned and am aware that many people looking at this book have far more local history knowledge than I have, so again I apologise for anything you find wrong or disagree with.

I have had just as much enjoyment preparing this book as I did with the first volume, so I hope you enjoy it as well.

Ann Beedham

Wingfield Manor

This book is dedicated to my brother Alan John Beedham. October 30th, 1944 - August 15, 2003

Abbeydale House

Just off busy Abbeydale Road, a once grand and secluded mansion house sits hidden and often unoticed, with its ornate stonework a resting place for pigeons.

On Barmouth Road, near Abbeydale Road's junction with Woodseats Road, is Abbeydale House. This lovely old building, once surrounded by countryside, is now crammed between houses, an antique centre and a car repair works.

Better Days

Abbeydale House was built in 1849 for John Rodgers, son of the Sheffield Industrialist of the famous firm Joseph Rodgers and Sons, who had a firm at 6 Norfolk Street. This firm built the amazing Norfolk Knife, shown below with an old ad for the firm.

JOSEPH RODGERS & SONS
LIMITED.

CUTLERS

By Special Appointment to Her Majesty,

6, NORFOLK ST., SHEFFIELD,
AND
No. 4, CULLUM STREET, FENCHURCH STREET,
LONDON, E.C.,

MERCHANTS, AND MANUFACTURERS OF

CUTLERY OF EVERY DESCRIPTION,

Silver and Plated Desserts, &c.

DEALERS IN SILVER,
BEST SHEFFIELD AND ELECTRO-PLATED WARES,
AND MOST OTHER ARTICLES OF SHEFFIELD MANUFACTURE.

The demand for J. R. and Sons' productions having considerably increased, they have, in order to meet it, greatly extended their Manufacturing Premises and Steam Power; and, for the convenience of Merchants and the Trade, now keep a large Stock of Cutlery at their London Establishment. They beg to caution the Public against spurious goods, offered by unprincipled houses, bearing their name and made to imitate their genuine Manufactures. A considerable quantity has been recently seized in the Port of London, and condemned by the Officers of Her Majesty's Customs.

To distinguish Articles of Joseph Rodgers and Sons' Manufacture, be careful to notice that they bear their Corporate Mark—thus

(CORPORATE ✳ ✧ MARK.)

The old residence is made in the Italian style, and was designed by architect Rooke Harrison.

It was said to be the most expensive one built in Sheffield at that time, and is rumoured to have cost around £30,000, an immense sum.

It stood in around six and a half acres of grounds, surrounded by lovely views. There were fountains, two spacious entrances, four large reception rooms, two kitchens, and twelve bedrooms. There was also a large wine cellar, with stone tables to store food and keep it cool.

Below, Abbeydale House, in an old print at Barmouth Court Antiques, surrounded by countryside

The house is sold

John Rodgers died just ten years after building this sumptuous home.

His nephew Robert Newbould took over the business and the house, then he built himself another house further up the road - Abbeydale Grange, now where the school of the same name stands.

Abbeydale House became unused and was auctioned, along with the lands. The surrounds were used for building and the city slowly engulfed the once isolated house.

JR- the initials of John Rodgers carved on the stairs

Old staircase in the house, now in ruins.

Detail from one of the pillars on Abbeydale House

In 1907 terraced houses, still there opposite the house today, were built. The wall of the house runs along their back yards. The old garden wall of the house can be traced along up Abbeydale Road, on the right, where coping stones can be spotted.

From the Sale catalogue

"Abbeydale House, near Sheffield, the residence of the late John Rodgers Esq.. Sale of the whole of the household furniture- from 1000--2000 ounces of solid silver..... curiosities...cabinet of specimens and articles of virtue...on Monday January 16 1860"

The sale took a week and more, with contents of the major rooms first then on the 8th day the stables and carriage house, the 9th day the wine cellar, the 10th day book engravings and caricatures.

An old view of Abbeydale House from Abbeydale Road, with the then newish terraced houses built alongside.

PHOTO: COURTESY OF SHEFFIELD CITY LIBRARY, LOCAL STUDIES ARCHIVES AND INFORMATION

The Snowite Laundry

Around 1903 the old house was bought by the Snowite Laundry. This well known Sheffield laundry was founded by a Mr W Bryars. Abbeydale House was their administrative headquarters.

The boardroom was on the first floor and was used until the 1960's. The laundry used Morris Oxford delivery vans, which were a familiar sight around Sheffield.

When the laundry left, the house was seen as superfluous and almost demolished. A frantic attempt to gain a restriction order to prevent the destruction of this historic building was eventually successful - a day after work to demolish it had begun. The house was saved, but it was too late to prevent the beautiful glass pagoda from being smashed, and the roof and chimneys being removed.

With no roof, the building, though now protected from destruction by human hand, was attacked by the elements. It Became more run down and was left empty at the mercy of wind and rain for 10 years.

It was eventually sold by the council. and bought privately. It passed on to an antique dealer called Norman Salt, who put on a new roof and took an interest in the old place, as well as using it as an occasional office extension to his nearby Barmouth Court Antiques Centre.

The antiques centre is housed in the old coach house of Abbeydale House. A balcony has been added to give another floor.

When Mr Salt purchased the place it was in a sorry state. He had to walk on a plank over gaping holes in the floor to inspect the property.

Local people told Mr Salt their memories and stories of his purchase. The area near the house is known as the 'lake district' and has streets named after this part of the country. One man told him a tale that there is an underground lake in the area, which is how it became named such. He said he remembered a bore hole being made in the coach house during the second world war, to provide fresh water when water supplies were disrupted due to bomb damage. Local people used the cellars of Abbeydale House as air raid shelters and amorous liaisons were said to have been frequent around the old place, under cover of the blackouts!

Today part of the old house is hidden in the workshop of Charlie Brown's motor workshops.

A narrow alley which runs down the side of nearby works Bee Brothers leads to the back of the old stables, down onto Carterknowle Road.

A photograph of the drivers from the Snowite Laundry, this was copied with kind permission of Mr Salt of Barmouth Court Antiques

More views of the old house

Above is a detail of the initials of John Rodgers above the staircase in the house.

Left: Pigeons rest on the old house

Right: the pathway to Carterknowle Road, past the old stable block

Barmouth Court Antiques Centre (0114 2552711), in the old coach house of Abbeydale House.

Also on Barmouth Road is this lovely old thirties style sign for the old Co-operative Society building

Endcliffe Hall

The grand and ornately decorated edifice of Endcliffe Hall

A large house, on Endcliffe Vale Road, Ranmoor, Sheffield, was once home to industrialist John Brown, one of the city's most wealthy, influential people...

In the busy Orchard Square shopping area, under the clock with it's grinder and buffer marking the hours, is a brass plaque commemorating a man named John Brown, who once had a workshop near that very spot.

Early Days

John Brown was born on December 6, 1816, at Favell's Yard, Fargate, near where Orchard Square shopping precinct now stands. He was the second son of Samuel Brown, a builder and slater and his wife Anne.

John decided he wanted to be a draper, and when he was 14 he was apprenticed to traders at Orchard Place.

In 1836 this firm moved into the steel trade, at Rockingham Street, making files and cutlery. John took a share in the business and worked taking samples of their work around.

He married an old school friend, Mary Schofield at Queen Street Chapel on September 4,1839.

John wanted to make his own cutlery, so he set up in Orchard Street in 1844.The business was a success and he moved to better premises at Furnival Street.

Maybe his days of travelling around with samples made him conscious of comfort on railway carriages, but for whatever reason, he began concentrating on railway buffers, rails etc.

It was also a boom time for building railways so a good business move. By 1848 he had invented the new idea of the 'conical steel railway buffers' said to make rail journeys less of a bumpy ordeal by improving the carriage suspension.

He expanded his business further, building converting furnaces for making blister steel in Holly Street. Railway springs and buffers were made in Upper Furnival Street.

In 1854 he moved all business to one site and purchased the Queens works on Savile Street.

He renamed it the Atlas works. It commenced production January 1 1856.

In 1856 Henry Bessemer invented his new process for making steel and set up next to Brown who soon was using this new steel, paying Bessemer a royalty of £1 a ton on steel rails. .

In 1860 Brown designed and built a rolling mill to make better armour plate.Brown won a gold award at the 1862 London Exhibition, for his work and became very well known.

In August 1862 Prime Minister Lord Palmerston visited Brown and saw armour plate made at the rolling mill. It was said at the time that three quarters of ironclads ships of the British Navy had Atlas Works plates. By 1867 the works covered 21 acres and had 4000 employees.

Brown became the first Sheffield steelmaker to be knighted.

"Another process which Messrs Brown and Co are carrying out is that of iron armour plates for war ships, for the manufacture of which the firm has become celebrated throughout the country. ...So extensive has become this branch of their manufacture that they are about to construct a mill specially for it and capable of turning out from 300 to 400 tons of finished plates weekly - twelve inches thick if necessary."

From Pawson and Braisford's Guide to Sheffield 1862

John Brown, from a bust at Kelham Island Museum, Sheffield. In the background are scenes of the Atlas Works

A Magnificent New Home

John Brown and his wife Mary were living at Shirle Hill, Sharrow, before they moved into their grand, specially built mansion named Endcliffe Hall in 1865. They had no children to fill the rooms, but lots of staff to take the space up!

Their hall was not the first on the site, however. Older buildings are mentioned in Joseph Hunter's 'Hallamshire' and also a merchant called Hodgson built a house around 1818, which later became known as Old Endcliffe Hall. This old hall was eventually sold to a Mr Henry Wilkinson, who owned it until 1863. That year the Hall and contents were sold by auction - by a firm called WH & JH Eadon.

The old Hall and its 25 acres were then bought up by John Brown, who demolished it and the outbuildings and built his new home on the site. Reporters visited the exciting and extravagant new mansion, which took less than two years to build.

The estimated cost was £100,000, not counting the furnishings, which came to another £60,000 or so. It would have cost around £14 million today.

Building, furniture and decorations were all designed in Sheffield and most of the work carried out by Sheffield craftspeople, which John Brown was justifiably proud of. The architects chosen for this new venture were Flockton and Abbott.

A Grand entrance

The main entrance was through the carriage porch at the east side of the hall. Past the lodge on Endcliffe Vale Road.

The drive up to the house was lit by ornamental gas lights, leading up to the grand carriage porch entrance.

Stone figures representing the seasons are on top of the porch. These are by artist E W Wyon. There are also two carved faces, possibly Victoria and Albert. As you enter, there is a **small conservatory** is on the left and a ballroom on the right.

The **ballroom** is the largest room in the house, around 60ft long and 39ft wide. In here were three large windows, over which could be wound mirrors hidden in wall cavities.

These and other windows in the hall also had exterior shutters which could be adjusted as sun blinds or to secure the place at night.

One remaining stove of the two that were in this room is shown left.

In this room there also used to be an organ. This was powered by water piped from a tank at the top of Endcliffe Vale Road.

A splendid staircase

There is a wonderful grand staircase at the hall, with the original Wrought iron balustrading and mahogany handrail. and a landing with lionhead carvings. Opposite this is one of the original marble fireplaces and a huge mirror. Gas light holders remain but now hold electric lights. There used to be decorated wall panels said to have been done by artist Godfrey Sykes (he has a monument in Weston Park).

1864 date carving from the main frontage

Example of an ornate ceiling of Endcliffe Hall, still splendid today

The grand staircase as it looks today

A Sumptuous Design Feast

The Layout

The ground floor of the hall had residential rooms and domestic rooms. The first floor had residential suites and bedrooms. A mezzanine floor was designed for servants bedrooms and bathrooms. The hall was also given a large tower, intended for use as a billiard room and observatory. There were three wine cellars and also small underground tunnels - probably built to hold the water or heating systems, perhaps for the long gone conservatory. There was also an elaborate electric bell system to call servants or announce a carriage arrival.

In the **main kitchen,** now offices, is the only survival from the old hall of 1863. This is a lovely naive animal carving of a hare and hound (above right).

The old **drawing room**, now used as a dining room, is a huge 31ft 6 by 28ft 6. The original fireplace, painted ceiling and door panels are still in place. The oval centre with figures that represent music painting and poetry is said to have been done by Godfrey Sykes.

Some original wallpaper with initials JB have been found during renovations and repairwork. Lots of drawings of the original furniture still survive in Sheffield City Archives, done for auction catalogues, when the hall was later sold.

The old **Morning Room** has solid mahogany doors. A shutter winding bar is still in the skirting under the windows- this enabled shutters to be wound in to be hidden in the wall.

The original white marble fireplace is still in place. A window looks into the **small conservatory.** This used to have paintings of Welsh views and steel window shutters.

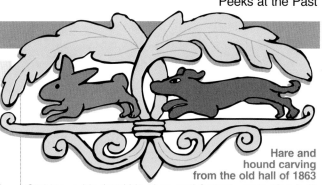

Hare and hound carving from the old hall of 1863

Stables, a blacksmith's shop and farmery were also built. Horses, cows and pigs were kept there. There also used to be a clock tower with a chiming clock in this area too. A laundry and accommodation for gardeners were also sited here. Another block used to hold a Turkish Bath and cooling room. To the right of the present entrance and near these old buildings is still a small marble drinking fountain with the date 1859.

The Conservatory

A huge conservatory, 160ft long and 35ft high used to stand in the grounds. It had a splendid dome and tower and was crammed with palms and exotic plants.

There was an elaborate series of plumbing to keep the plants warm by piping hot water nearby. This magnificent glasshouse was later used as a hospital (see over the page).

Scrollwork on the exterior have initials of businesses involved in building the hall:

C B Bros (Craven Brothers - builders

F & AA (Flockton and Abbott- architects

M&I Sc (Mawer and Ingle - stonecarvers (above)

Outside The Hall

The hall was once surrounded by 40 acres of grounds, laid out by the architect Flockton. The estate was bounded by Fulwood Road Riverdale Road and Endcliffe Vale Road.

There were formal Italian gardens. Also there were fountains, an ornamental lake and a pond. There was a reservoir for these at the corner of Endcliffe Vale Road and Fulwood Road. (It was filled in during the 1930's).

Exterior carvings

A carved date of 1864 graces the main frontage. Brown was granted a coat of arms in 1868, when he was knighted. It comprises of a lion, a beehive (for industriousness?), a star and a coil (this represents the conical steel railway spring buffer which made his fame). His motto was NEC SORTE NEC FATO (Neither by chance nor destiny) - probably meaning he had worked hard for what he had, not got it easily.

The coat of arms can be seen on the exterior shot of the main frontage (left). This frontage also has on top two carved figures, by a sculptor called Papworth, they symbolise Labour and art. Labour is unfortunately now headless.

A large beehive with bees in stonework is found adjacent to the carriage porch. (see right).

John Brown's coat of arms

Most of the ground floor window sills have elaborate carvings, for example fruit, flowers and a birds nest complete with eggs.

Drawing room bay windows have faces, a rose, a shamrock and a thistle and swords from the arms of the Cutlers' company. (John Brown was made Master Cutler in 1865- briefly - due to illness, then re-elected in 1866). He was also Lord Mayor in 1861.

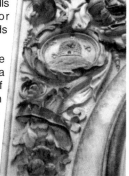

A beehive, from the porch

The House is Auctioned

John Brown lived at Endcliffe Hall for about 30 years. His wife Mary died in 1881, and as his own health deteriorated, he began to spend more time away down south.

With John Brown away so often, in 1892 the contents of the hall were sold, put in the hands of London firm of auctioneers. There was a grand catalogue listing the sumptuous contents and furnishings.

Sheffield City Council were asked if they wanted to buy the hall, for an amazing bargain price of £70,000, less than half of the money spent on building and furnishing it. Ideas were mooted that it could be turned into a convalescent home, a library, an orphanage or the Council

Right: One of the lion head carvings from the landing of the main staircase

Coat of arms on one of the walls

were not interested, thinking it would be a big white elephant.

Maple and Co. were the ones who sold all of the contents of the hall at their grand auction, which lasted for five days, from 17 - 21 April 1893. Every single item was listed in the huge catalogue, even down to garden tools. Many things were sold for well below the expected value and there were many bargains to be had.

ENDCLIFFE HALL ESTATE, NEAR SHEFFIELD,
The Property and until lately the Residence of Sir John Brown, Knight.

Plans, Particulars & Conditions of Sale
OF THE VERY
VALUABLE and MAGNIFICENT

FREEHOLD MANSION

KNOWN AS

"ENDCLIFFE HALL,"

AT SHEFFIELD, IN THE COUNTY OF YORK,
WITH THE
Conservatories, Gardens, Stabling, Laundry, Farmery, &c.

The Site of the whole contains 33a. 1r. 30p., and the Park and Lands are exceedingly valuable for Building purposes

TO BE SOLD BY AUCTION,

BY MESSRS.

NICHOLSON, GREAVES, BARBER & HASTINGS,

AT THEIR

ESTATE SALE ROOM, 46, HIGH ST., SHEFFIELD,

ON

TUESDAY, the 30th day of JULY, 1895,

AT FOUR O'CLOCK P.M.

Subject to the following Special Conditions, and to the General Conditions of Sale of the Sheffield District Incorporated Law Society.

The Property presents many most attractive Building Sites and is beautifully wooded. The Estate is about Two miles from the Parish Church of Sheffield.

For Plans, Particulars and further information, and for Cards of Permission to View the Property, apply to Messrs. FLOCKTON & GIBBS, Architects and Surveyors, St. James' Row, Sheffield; the AUCTIONEERS; or to

HENRY VICKERS, SON AND BROWN,
SOLICITORS,
North Street, SHEFFIELD

The hall itself, with over 33 acres of land, was sold at another auction on July 30 1895 (see the advertising leaflet above).

It sold for about £26,000, to a syndicate of local businessmen. They formed the Endcliffe Estates Company and built new roads around the hall, as well as more fine buildings.

Endcliffe Hall itself was used for dances, parties, exhibitions and special events.

John Brown died on 27th December 1896, at a friend's home in Kent. His body was returned to Sheffield and buried alongside Mary at Ecclesall Church.

PHOTOGRAPH CORTESY OF SHEFFIELD LOCAL STUDIES LIBRARY

A photograph of the interior at Endcliffe Hall, showing the wealth of paintings, sculptures, and fittings that were sold off

Opening and Auction Publicity

From the Maple & Co Ltd auction guide:

All that very valuable freehold estate, known as
"The Endcliffe Hall Estate," Sheffield, with the magnificent
Mansion thereon. called "Endcliffe Hall," erected by Sir John
Brown, Knight, with beautifully laid-out Gardens and
Grounds, handsome Conservatories, excellent Stabling with
every requirement, Farmery.
Laundry &c. Very productive Kitchen Garden.

This is one of the most charming properties in the
neighbourhood of SHEFFIELD, as it occupies a grand
position on the summit of a hall, surrounded by good hard
roads, possesses views (extending to the Moors) of great
beauty, is within an easy walk of the Town and
distant only three miles from principal Railway Stations.
It is thus especially suitable for a wealthy Manufacturer or
Merchant, or it would form a splendid Public Park or Building
Estate as it has about 3,000 feet frontage to the FULWOOD
and ENDCLIFFE VALE ROADS.

Built for the present owner and planned in a most
successful manner, so as to combine the attractions of an
imposing Mansion with the comforts of a pleasant home; it is
decorated in an elaborate and costly manner and the
various fittings are of the most costly character.

The windows are plate glass and those of the Reception
Rooms are fitted in massive mahogany frames, while the
principal windows on the Ground Floor are protected by
sliding steel shutters, with plate-glass panels and the
Mansion and Conservatories are heated throughout by hot
air and water pipes, with a large stone chimney to carry
away the smoke of the furnaces.

Below: A newspaper article about Endcliffe Hall opening

SHEFFIELD, YORKSHIRE.

Situate on high ground in the residential part of the Borough, three miles from the Midland and Manchester and Sheffield Railway Stations.

Particulars

OF A CHARMING

Freehold Residential Estate,

KNOWN AS

ENDCLIFFE HALL,

COMPRISING A

NOBLE & ADMIRABLY ARRANGED FAMILY MANSION

(IN THE ITALIAN STYLE OF ARCHITECTURE).

Built for the present owner in 1864, in an excellent state of repair, replete with every comfort, and upon which large amounts have been lavishly expended in the internal Appointments and Decorations, which are of a most handsome and costly description.

IT IS

Seated well within beautifully arranged Pleasure Grounds, of a very ornamental character, adorned with finely grown Forest Timber and Coniferæ, and including Italian Garden, Terrace (asphalted walks), with Ornamental Water and Fountains, extensive Lawns, Rosery, Shrubberies, etc., and approached from North and South by lengthy winding Carriage Drives, with

HANDSOME LODGE ENTRANCES.

In the rear of the Mansion and built in the form of a quadrangle is the

EXTENSIVE STABLING, FARMERY & LAUNDRY,

WITH

Large Walled Kitchen Garden,

A

GRAND CONSERVATORY 160 FEET IN LENGTH,

WITH OTHER GLASS HOUSES,

AND

The Well-Timbered Undulating Park,

The whole containing about THIRTY-FIVE ACRES.

POSSESSION WILL BE GIVEN ON COMPLETION OF PURCHASE.

MAPLE & CO LTD.,

Have been favoured with instructions to sell this choice Estate by private treaty, and printed Particulars with Photos, together with orders to view, can be obtained at their Offices,

TOTTENHAM COURT ROAD, LONDON, W.;

AND

EASTBOURNE, SUSSEX.

SHEFFIELD DAILY TELEGRAPH, WEDNESDAY MAY 24, 1865

ENDCLIFFE HALL,
THE PUBLIC ADVANTAGE OF PERSONAL MUNIFICENCE

... "our merchant princes are beginning to house themselves like princes, in palaces; ...the new aristocracy which trade and commerce are daily increasing in numbers and power. David Baxter, Frank Crossley, William Brown, Titus Salt, James Peabody and one John Brown, as well as others in Sheffield, are men who have won their present positions by right of that best of all competitive examinations- the rough and searching competitive examination of the conflict of business ...These men are something more than dilettante patrons of sculptors and artists. Their business wants have called our Schools of Art into existence and their personal taste, associated with their well earned wealth, has needed the best work of those schools for the adornment of their abodes.

...on the walls of Endcliffe they are engaged in bringing out those tones and undertones of colour which illustrate their mastery of chromatic harmonies. Most admirably is the tinting of the ceilings....One pleasing feature...is the way in which Ruskin's idea of relying on the innate beauty of buildings and furnishing materials is being worked out. The tiled floors clean as biscuit porcelain, the glazed bricks looking like blocks of cream coloured China, the natural oak smoothed and polished until its tone and grain come out under the polish like the work of the lapidary....

The arrangements for saving labour are so numerous and ingenious that we shall not attempt to describe them. The exterior of the building is of commanding proportions and being well placed...its windows show from the inside like so many framed pictures in which each frame gives a different landscape view. Some very fine sculpture adorns the front of the edifice and the terraces and the drives are adorned with numerous lamps..."

ARCHITECTURAL DETAILS

The name of Endcliffe Hall has long being familiar in Sheffield and is now especially noteworthy because the old building so long known by the name has now passed away and given place to a new mansion of rare architectural beauties and proportions worthy of the charming and varied landscapes of the locality in which it is situated. Mr. Alderman John Brown, the proprietor, employed Messrs. Flockton and Abbott to design and carry out the mansion almost regardless of cost and those gentlemen have succeeded in producing a building which, for perfect architecture, excellent workmanship, unique domestic arrangement and appropriate accessories, cannot, we think be surpassed in the provinces...

The park in which the house is situated embraces a considerable portion of Endcliffe Wood and has an extent altogether of about 40 acres, enclosed on its principal side by a low wall and beautiful pallisading. The hall is approached by a principal and a secondary gateway, the first of which is at the tower end, where there is a handsome lodge. From the lodge the carriage drive leads to the entrance front... The principal feature of this front, the carriage porch, is formed by the end of the house conservatory and the side of the saloon and is decorated with four groups of statuary representing the four seasons.

TERRACES, GARDENS, &c.- In addition to the entrance terrace the house stands upon an upper terrace, from which a numerous flight of steps lead down to a large flat terrace garden...Upon the upper terrace are several small ornamental fountains and in the centre of the lower portion preparation is made for a large fountain. The lower terrace garden is bounded on the north by a range of conservatories and a pavilion of stone and glass at each end, with an octagonal one in the centre, surmounted with a lofty dome.

A new role for the grand old residence

Picture courtesy of Local Studies, Sheffield Libraries, Archives and Information

The conservatory being used as a hospital in the First World War. Nurses and beds are just visible.

In 1913 there were plans to demolish the hall and use the land. This was greeted with protests and schemes were talked over by local gentlemen to pay rent towards hiring the hall, which they considered a valuable local amenity, and so paying for it's upkeep.

This was never done, however, as an alternative offer for purchasing the hall was put in by one Colonel GE Branson.

One of the ceiling paintings at Endcliffe Hall, still to be seen now the house has a new role

He was applying to buy it on behalf of West Riding Territorial Force Association. He wanted the hall to replace the old Hyde Park Barracks as headquarters for the Hallamshire Battalion.

This idea was approved and so the hall was sold to the Association in January 1914. The hall was altered to prepare it for it's new role and the stables and coach house were converted into a drill hall.

In the First World War (1914-1918), the soldiers whose headquarters were now Endcliffe Hall were fighting in France.

Endcliffe Hall became a hospital for military casualties, as the 3rd Northern General Hospital. Mark Firth's old home of Oakbrook nearby (now Notre Dame School) was used too..

120 patients were housed here, with nurses. There were eight wards and also an outdoor ward which was in the conservatory. Glass was removed from the conservatory to do this.

In 1919 electric light was installed at the hall. Many more alterations and modernisations were carried out in 1984. The gardens had been levelled in the 1920s to make a parade ground.

In 1989, on 9th June, her Royal Highness the Duchess of Kent visited the Hall. John Brown had always wanted royalty to visit his home and was said to have had been very annoyed when Victoria and Albert visited his rival Mark Firth at his nearby home at Oakbrook instead. Perhaps he was looking on in approval to see a royal visit at last.

The Territorial Army are still the owners of Endcliffe Hall today, under the name of Yorkshire and Humberside RFCA (Reserved Forces Cadet Association) and there is no public access.

It is, however, possible for groups to arrange guided tours of the hall. Telephone 0114 2663242 for further information.

These photographs are from the Sheffield Newspapers Archive

Endcliffe Hall in the 1980's

A royal visit from the Duchess of Kent in June 1989

10

Fulwood Inn

View of the inn from the car park

Along Fulwood Road and not far from the old Endcliffe Hall, stands another fine old mansion built for a Sheffield Industrialist, now used as a public house...

This huge old house stands proud above the elegant Fulwood Road. Some of the grounds are now a car park and give a fine view of the building.

A magnificent home

The Fulwood Inn was originally a private residence. It was built for the wealthy steel industrialist James Nicholson, who named it Moordale.

The building has also been home to the National Coal Board and then a computer company.

Grand entrance

Over the main door is the latin motto "Malum Bono Vince" which can roughly be translated as 'Good conquers Bad'.

There is also a grotesque fanged monster face and a decorated archway The outside of the building has some lean looking winged dragon gargoyles. **Right is the ornate motto carving on the doorway (below)**

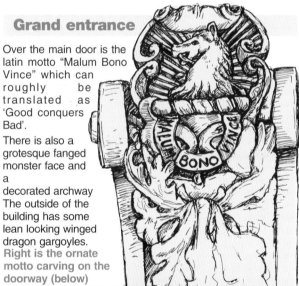

Below is a lovely arch from the interior and also the fanged monster from the doorway. Right is a gargoyle

Last resting place

James Nicholson is buried in the General Cemetery at Sharrow. The family monument is one of the loveliest in the cemetery, featuring a kneeling woman in prayer. It used to have angels at its corners, but they have been lost.

The monument commemorates James, and other members of the family, including Harriet Nicholson who died in 1876, Her husband, who commissioned the monument and died in 1909, is also buried there, as are their children.

The location of the monument is shown on the map, right.

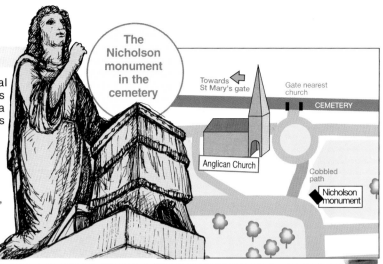

The Nicholson monument in the cemetery

Towards St Mary's gate

Gate nearest church

CEMETERY

Anglican Church

Cobbled path

Nicholson monument

Around the Fulwood Inn

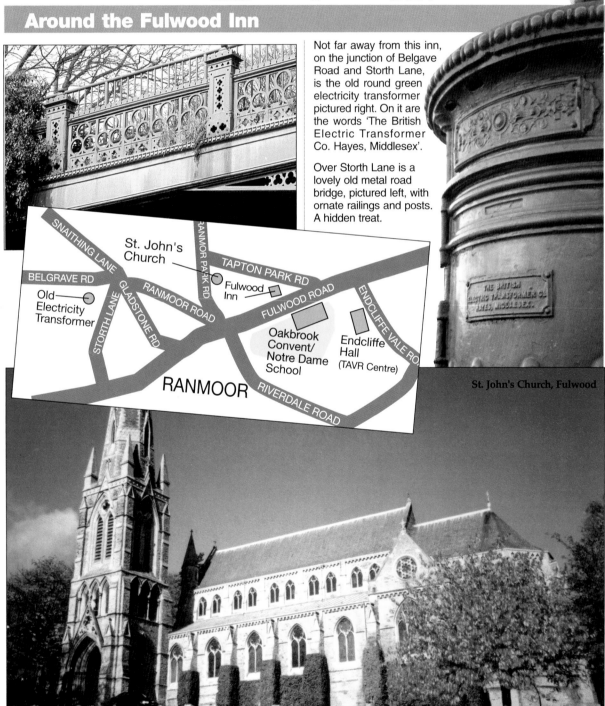

Not far away from this inn, on the junction of Belgave Road and Storth Lane, is the old round green electricity transformer pictured right. On it are the words 'The British Electric Transformer Co. Hayes, Middlesex'.

Over Storth Lane is a lovely old metal road bridge, pictured left, with ornate railings and posts. A hidden treat.

SNAITHING LANE

RANMOOR PARK RD

St. John's Church

TAPTON PARK RD

BELGRAVE RD

GLADSTONE RD

RANMOOR ROAD

Fulwood Inn

FULWOOD ROAD

ENDCLIFFE VALE RD

Old Electricity Transformer

STORTH LANE

Oakbrook Convent/ Notre Dame School

Endcliffe Hall (TAVR Centre)

RANMOOR

RIVERDALE ROAD

THE BRITISH ELECTRIC TRANSFORMER CO. HAYES, MIDDLESEX

St. John's Church, Fulwood

St Matthew's Church

St Matthew's Church, on Carver Street in the city centre

Squashed in between the newer buildings around Division Street, Sheffield, on Carver Street, and once surrounded by slums, is a lovely old church with a turbulent past...

St Matthew's is a hidden gem, its spire rising over car parks, pizza restaurants and wine bars, it is time capsule of art and tradition, now a spiritual beacon for the busy city centre. It is the only Anglo Catholic, tradition church in the region.

The first hundred years

Saint Matthew's was built when the Anglican Cathedral was still the parish church of Sheffield.

The first vicar of St Matthew's was the Reverend J F Witty. He had helped raise money for the church, the foundation stone of which was laid on June 1st, 1854.

The church was consecrated on June 6, 1855, by the Archbishop of York. The building and land had cost £3,775.

Father Ommanney

The history of St Matthew's is closely tied into that of Reverend George Campbell Ommanney. He was vicar of the church from 1882 until his death on March 10, 1936.

He was from an Oxfordshire military family and came to Sheffield at the age of 32, with nine years experience as a curate at Oxford and Bristol, but was soon at odds with his congregation at St Matthew's because of his views.

Under his guidance St Matthew's became one of the most famous churches of the Catholic Revival in England. It was and is, well known for being Anglo Catholic, or High Church - Anglican, but with strong Catholic links.

This type of high church worship was considered by many of the parishioners to be too ritualistic and close to 'Popish practices'. The unrest even led to several brawls in the church. Outbursts during services led to worshippers being ejected.

The complaints against Ommanney included the fact that he used wafers instead of bread for communion, that he used a server or acolyte and that he used an embroidered chalice veil.

St Matthew's in earlier days

Photo: From the Star Archives

Ommanney also got rid of the small table that had been used as an altar, and had it replaced with a more imposing altar with frontals and candles.

The vicar's warden, a Mr Wynn, was very opposed to Father Ommanney's ways and duly replaced, which he took badly.

Wynn complained to the Archbishop of York and in 1883, there were many letters and disapproving words from the Bishop to Ommanney, but to no avail, as Ommanney only slightly altered his ways.

Trouble broke out again in 1900, when a group, led by a Mr Kensit, interrupted a service and protested against the 'idolatry', which resulted in a scuffle. In 1912 the 'Kensit-ites' took statues from the church to the Archbishop's Palace at York. A year later, a statue was smashed in the church.

As well as being a controversial man, Ommanney was well loved as a man who was a champion of the poor, campaigning for better sanitary conditions and housing.

Almost lost

The church survived the Sheffield Blitz in the Second World War, being 'blacked out' so people could still worship. Much of the area around it was lost or damaged though.

In August 1956 it was again in danger, this time by a fire, which damaged the organ, ruined choir vestments and damaged the Lady Chapel which had been added only two weeks before.

Much refurbishment was carried out after this, making the church less gloomy. Much of the money for this was raised by an appeal from the church to industry, for contributions.

In the seventies, the church was again threatened, this time by council redevelopment, but plans were changed to keep the church and its buildings, and on the same site.

A rift healed

Because of his ways of worship, Father Ommanney had been placed under discipline in 1898, which meant that no Bishops were allowed to visit St Matthew's. This ban was not lifted until 1931.

In July 1998, the Archbishop of York, Dr David Hope, made a historic visit to St Matthew's, the first time an Archbishop had been in the church since it was consecrated. He also launched an appeal for £350,000 to restore the building.

Inside St Matthew's Church

Relics

In 1984, when the church was having building work done inside, an old chalice (cup used for wine in a mass service) and paten (plate used for bread or wafers in a mass service) were found. Both were blackened by age and were thought to be the originals from when the church was first built.

They were polished and sent to Africa (Burundi) after an appeal for old church altar plate, to be used in a church there.

Piscina

By the door, on the left of the porch is a water container, or *piscina,* for holy water, with a cross above and the latin words In Hoc Signo Vinces - in this sign (the cross) conquer.

The High Altar

This was designed by an architect called John Sedding. He also designed the lovely candlesticks, crucifix and processional cross that are used in the services. These are catalogued in the Victoria and Albert Museum.

The altar itself is made from oak, inlaid with copperwork depicting the worship of heaven from the Revelation of St John.

The reredos (back altar screen) has recently been restored, as has the recently restored Pre-Raphaelite painting of the nativity which decorates it. (see panel right). The figures on the reredos are St Henry, St Lawrence, St Anne, and St Crispin.

Other chapels in the church are the Sacred Heart Chapel (left of the central High Altar), The lady Chapel, (right of the High Altar) and St George's chapel (on the right wall of the church as you enter). There are lovely statues at each of these

Windows

The window on the right of the door looking from the altar is dedicated to 20 years of work by Rev Ommanney and was given by William Crompton, his warden for 9 years, in June 1902. The signature of the makers, Lavers and Westlake of London and the date 1902 can be seen in the bottom right hand corner.

The signature of the same makers can be seen in the window on the other side of the door, again at bottom right.

The pulpit

The Pulpit

Dedicated to the memory of Walter Weekes, an assistant priest, who died on February 15, 1902, aged 30. There are lovely copper panels which tell of the dedication.

The font

The Font

This is dedicated to the memory of Octavius Ommanney, who died on July 30, 1901 and also Helen Ommanney, who died on New Years Eve, 1894.

A rediscovered treasure

Father Simon Griffiths with the restored painting

The painting on the reredos altar screen of the high altar was for years hidden beneath layers of grime. It had never been varnished and dirt, including soot and smoke from incense and candles, built up on it's surface, hiding the true beauty and subject matter and value of the piece.

The painting was cleaned by local experts during 2002, with help from English Heritage lottery funding.

When the cleaning was underway, a signature and date previously hidden revealed it is by Pre - Raphaelite artist Nathaniel Westlake, who painted it in 1890. It depicts a nativity scene.

It was placed back in position in early 2003, restored to its former, bright coloured glory. The reredos frame was also re-gilded and the painting was given a coat of conserving glaze to protect it.

Altar cloth colours

The altar is dressed in a different colour cloth, reflecting the time of the church year.

WHITE is for the most important occasions as it is the purest colour. Used at Christmas and Easter.

RED is for Saint's days, reflecting blood spilt by martyrs. Also used on Palm Sunday

GREEN is for any other day

PURPLE is the royal colour, used at advent and lent, working up to the most important days.

BLACK is the colour of death, used at funerals.

At Easter the altar is left bare. Also the crucifixes will be covered up.

This statue of the Virgin Mary stands by the Lady Chapel

Angels

These two angels at prayer face each other on the walls just in front of the high altar, above the choir stalls

There are some lovely 'stations of the cross' along the walls of St Matthew's. These depict the journey of Christ to his crucifixion.

St Matthew's organ

The organ

The splendid organ of St Matthew's is a hidden musical gem in the city. It was built and installed by the Nottinghamshire firm of Goetze and Gwynn in 1992, to replace an older one.

It is a copy of a mid-17th century instrument (Baroque style) built by a German organ builder called Bernhard Schmidt, who settled in England in 1666.

This one however has an electric means of providing the wind power, instead of using people to operate bellows!

It is used at services and also for occasional recitals.

There is also an established choir at St Matthews, which would welcome new members.

The Rood

The rood (an old name for cross) is in memory of the Rev. George Campbell Ommanney and was dedicated on 11 August 1946, by Kenneth the Bishop of Oxford.

Bishop Kirk was brought up at St Matthew's under Father Ommanney.

Choir screens

The iron screens at the back of the choir seats are copies of those in Pisa cathedral. They were made locally.

Characterful carvings on the choir stalls

These carvings of animals and plants are on the seats for the choir. Look out for the owl, otter, mouse, woodpecker and squirrel.

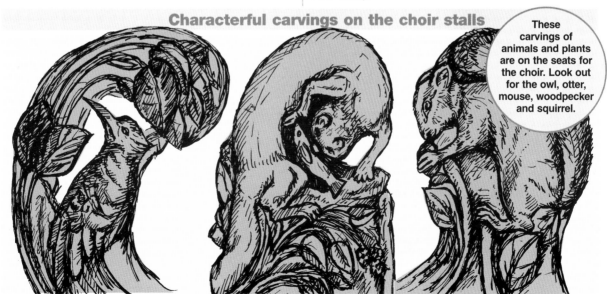

The crucifixion statue outside the church was added later as a war memorial.

The carved heads shown right are to be found on either side of the main entrance door of the church

A sketch of the interior of St Matthew's church, looking towards the altar.

Location and services

Services at St Matthews

SUNDAY:	9am	Mass
	11am	Solemn Mass
	6.30pm	Evening Prayer and Benediction

WEEKDAYS:	12.30pm	Mass (Mon, Tues, Wed, Fri)
	6.30pm	Mass (Thurs)

SATURDAY:	8.30am	Mass

■ For further information contact the vicar, Simon Griffiths on 0114 2305641

■ If you are a singer or organist and want to join in with the musical tradition at St Matthews, ring the church for details

Above is Carver Street today, with the spire of St. Matthews soaring above the street, a hidden gem amongst the shops restaurants and bars

This lovely angel shown below can be found on St Matthew's House, to the right of the church

On and near Carver Street

Near St. Matthew's, on the other side of Carver Street, dissected by Division Street, is an old school. The sign near the roofline reads " **National School. Built by subscription in 1812.** It is now a wine bar called Dikkins.

Almost opposite here is a lovely old sign on a building called Alpha House, at number 10.

The sign above number 10

The old sign on the right can be found on Cambridge Street, opposite the John Lewis (formerly Cole Brothers) store. It is on old gates that front a yard full of old workshops, now awaiting a new fate and currently empty. The place is called Leah's Yard, after the old stamping works that used to be there.

JOHN MANUEL & SON

Are prepared to remove with their FIRST-CLASS VANS, by Rails or Road, every description of Furniture, Pictures, Glass and Goods requiring care, in all cases sending thorough, efficient and experienced workmen.

They have also added extensive premises which they have fitted up for Warehousing Furniture, Pictures, &c.; the whole being effectively heated by means of hot water pipes.

Devonshire Cabinet Works,

UPHOLSTERY,

CARPET AND GENERAL PUBLIC SHOW ROOMS,

DIVISION STREET & CARVER STREET,

SHEFFIELD.

187

JOHN MANUEL AND SON,

Upholsterers

and

Carpet Warehousemen;

MANUFACTURERS OF

EVERY DESCRIPTION OF

CABINET FURNITURE,

DEVONSHIRE CABINET WORKS,

39 and 41, Division Street;

29 and 31, Carver Street,

SHEFFIELD.

ESTIMATES SUPPLIED FREE FOR COMPLETE HOUSE FURNISHING

The old advertisements above, from the old Pawson and Brailsford's guide to Sheffield are for a coach building firm that used to be on Carver Street and Devonshire Street, now long gone.

There were also dentists on Carver Street in the 1890's, advertised in the same old guide: At number 16 and advertised as 'opposite the National Schools' was Mr Henry Bower, Surgeon Dentist. At number 9 was another- Mr Brindley.

Was he a relation to Charles Brindley, organ builder, on the same street at number 30, next to St Matthew's? Could be a disaster if a person went to the wrong one!

At number 49 Carver Street was Spencer and Atherton's powder and dram bottles shop and at number 75 was G & J W Hawksley, 'sporting implements, breech loading and muzzle loading guns.'

The Water Works Building

This lovely old building is near to St Matthews, on Division Street, on the left hand side of the City Hall. It was built in 1867 for The Sheffield Water Company and their name is still carved on the frontage. The building was from a design by the architects Flockton and Abbot.

Right is one of the carved heads from the front of the building. This one is in the centre, over the main doorway

The company was in the hands of the city council by 1887 and later it became the home of J G Graves' mail order business. He was very wealthy and also generous and is the same Graves who gave the Art Gallery and also the the Park bearing his name to the city.

Now the old building is a bar / restaurant but still retains its feeling of grandeur, as you walk up the steps and through the huge doors.

Wharncliffe Fireclay

Near St Matthew's, on Devonshire Street, is a building covered in a riot of carvings. Flora and faces adorn the facadé, which was once a showroom for a fireclay works

On the busy, shop filled Devonshire Street in the centre of Sheffield, opposite the green space of Devonshire Green, is a lovely old building that is like a work of art, a sampler of the sculptor's talent.

Clay workings

In the late 19th century, clay was used to make the crucible pots for Benjamin Huntsman's steel process, as well as for lining furnaces.

The particular type of clay in the area good for this was from the Deepcar area, and was known as fireclay. The Deepcar area was worked for clay until as late as the 1990's.

A man called John Armitage was a dealer in the clay business and specialised in decorated, figures tiles and ornamentation made from it.

Some of the decorative work on the building

The name and date on John Armitage's showroom

Decorations

John Armitage opened his factory with showroom on Devonshire Street in 1888, to demonstrate the range and quality of his products.

Even the building was used as one big advertisement, which is why it is so highly decorated.

An artist called Peter Nanetti designed the bricks and carvings.

The two roundels with faces are to be found on the side of the building. Below is the Armitage name and a flower tile

This whiskered old face is to be seen near the front of the building

Abbeydale Cinema

The striking white dome of the Abbeydale Picture House

This once proud cinema dominates a site on Abbeydale Road, its dome seen from afar over the city as it waits to see what the future holds...

The Abbeydale Picture House opened on December 20, 1920. It was a favourite spot for Sheffielder's to head to see the old silent films.

A grand new venue

The striking white building which stands on Abbeydale Road, was designed by architects Dixon and Steinlet of North Shields, with a man called Arthur Whitaker supervising.

It stands out brightly like some kind of Florentine church, with its classical style and white surface, which is made from faience tile cladding. There is a domed tower and balustrade above the main entrance and the word 'Cinema' in white tile letters. At the side is a smaller entrance.

Originally there was a stained glass canopy along the building and one over the side entrance, to shelter people as they came and went. or queued up. These have now gone, but the old holders for the canopy struts can still be seen along the wall, on the same level as the bottom of the windows.

The Abbeydale Picture House, as this lovely old place used to be, was officially opened by the Lord Mayor of Sheffield.

It was a grand and decadent place to see and be seen. There was a cafe at balcony level and the basement had a billiard hall and later a ballroom, which opened in September 1921 and remained popular for many years, especially through the Second World War.

From the Sheffield Independent, Saturday, 18 December, 1920

A SUPER-CINEMA

Lord Mayor to Open New Sheffield Theatre

Sheffield's newest supercinema, the Abbeydale Picture House, is to be opened on Monday by the Lord Mayor of Sheffield Alderman W.F.Wardley, with the Lady Mayoress, the Countess Fitzwilliam, Lady Mary Wharncliffe and Lord Milton as patrons.

The new hall will be one of the finest in the provinces and the largest in Sheffield. While it is exceptionally lofty and spacious, the proprietors' ideas are more in the direction of providing comfort than seating accommodation. It is a model in this line of furnishing.

The "Last Word"

Everything about the place represents the present-day "last word" in this class of theatre - the newest machinery, an exceptionally large screen, the latest methods of heating and ventilation. By a special plant, hot or cold air, as conditions demand, will be driven through all parts of the house, thus ensuring 'purity' of atmosphere.

The musical side of the programme will be very attractive and Mr Arnold Bagshaw, as director of an orchestra of ten members, will have as his object "playing to the pictures" rather than with them.

Billiard and Ball Rooms

A large room below the theatre is to be equipped as a high-class billiard saloon, and a ballroom, with permanent spring floor, is to be another of the attractions at this wonder cinema. Cafe accommodation is also to be a feature.

A view of the cinema from over Abbeydale Road

Details of the building

One of the windows, with decorative carved tile foliage

NEW CINEMA THEATRE

LORD MAYOR OPENS ABBEYDALE PICTURE PALACE

Reported to be one of the finest halls in the provinces and the biggest in Sheffield, The Abbeydale Picture Palace was opened yesterday afternoon by the Lord Mayor (Alderman W.F. Wardley). There was a large attendance and additional interest was given to the function by the fact that the proceeds were to be devoted to Sheffield medical charities.

The theatre has accommodation for about 1,800 persons and is spacious and lofty, with a beautifully arched ceiling. The design is of classic style and is carried out in pale and deep cream with gold.

At the side of the screen are two Doric pillars and over the top a chaste panel of Grecian figures on a background of pale blue.

The seats are most comfortable and are upholstered in green velvet with mahogany fittings. .....

.....At one time, plush chairs were to be seen only in the King's box in one of the theatres in London. Now the working people could have one to sit in after their day's work.

This stained glass, with its beaming star design, is found in the windows of the dome.

From the Sheffield Independent, Tuesday, 21 December, 1920

It was a large cinema, holding around 1,560 people. The interior was very plush and probably a very luxurious experience for the working people of Sheffield- a treat of a night out. The screen had a proscenium arch, like a theatre.

On either side of it were Doric pillars like a Greek temple and above was a frieze of Grecian figures on a background of pale blue. These were covered up in 1954 when a larger panoramic screen was added.

The decor was a deep cream with gold embelishments. The very swish seats had mahogany fittings and were covered with green velvet.

The film shows

The first event at the Abbeydale Picture House was a charity event.The film was 'The Call of The Wild'. The newspaper advertisement declared it "A picture that will make history." No indication as to why though.

The film show played twice nightly and ticket prices were 2/- (10p), 1/3 (6p), 9d (4p), and 6d (2.5p).

In December 1928, a new and better stage was built and dressing rooms improved to make variety shows more viable at the cinema. This never took off though, as a new development was all the rage instead - the Talkies.

Talking pictures arrived at Abbeydale in April 1930, with a new sound system being installed to accommodate this new exciting development in cinema going. The first talkie there was 'Sunny Side Up'.

The cinema was later taken over by the Star Cinema group, in 1950. They introduced Sunday opening and the popular Saturday childrens matinees.

Not long after, in 1955 another new invention, 'cinemascope' arrived, the first film in the new format being Seven Brides for Seven Brothers.

A decorative cupola on the cinema roof, perhaps to provide air flow

One of the exterior decorative features

End of the reels

The last reels flickered for the old film venue on July 5, 1975.The final films shown were 'Breakout' starring Charles Bronson and one called 'The Lords of Flatbush'.

After that it became premises for Drakes, office furniture sellers, until 1991.

There have been various bars and concerts in the place too and there is a snooker hall underneath which still operates.

At time of writing the old cinema is awaiting a possible new fate as a performing and visual arts centre.

Friends of The Abbeydale Picture House formed in 2003 to 'purchase, renovate, develop and manage' the place. Their aim is to turn it into a community centre for performing arts and visual media and to promote the educational and community capacity of the building.

This would be a good use of a fine old building that deserves to be preserved in all it's grandness.

The lavishly decorated interior of the cinema house

A view from the top of Heeley Millennium Park, showing how the old cinema stands out amongst the other buildings

Far left is a view of the side of the Abbeydale Picture House, taken from the car park.

Left s one of the old rings to which the ties for the canopy were attached. Even they have some ornate scrollwork. Below is a location map.

To city centre

ABBEYDALE ROAD

NETHER EDGE

Abbeydale Picture House

BROADFIELD RD

Stokes Paints (Mazeppa carving)

LITTLE LONDON

CHESTERFIELD ROAD

Brindley, the organ builder

There was an orchestra of 10 musicians at the cinema, until a 'Clavorchester' organ was installed in 1921. This organ was made by the firm of Brindley and Foster at the Suffolk Road Workshops (see below). The opening of the new organ at the cinema was held on 31st October 1921. A famous musician and musical director at the time, a Mr Arthur Meale, was at the keyboards that night, especially visiting from London.

Mr Arnold Bagshaw was the leader of the resident orchestra and was later resident organist there. The "Programme of Pictures" for the night included "The Pathe Gazette, Picta Jokes (humour in verse, prose and pictures), and the Bray Pictograph (contains so much that is interesting, instructive and amusing."

Charles Brindley was born in Baslow in 1833. He made his living as a bell hanger at first, but by 1841 he had moved to Sheffield and began new work as an organ builder.

By 1862 he had a business at 30 Carver Street, next to St. Matthew's church. He was very successful and later, in 1865, expanded into premises at 33 Carver Street. These old work places are now long gone and built over.

A couple of years later, Brindley went into a partnership with another organ builder called Albert Healy Foster. In 1867 they moved to new premises at the junction of Columbia Place and Fornham Street, which fronted onto Suffolk Road.

The building was called Colombia Place and had originally been built as a steel and file works in 1849, by a man called Thomas Tillotson.Then it had three storeys, but the top storey was removed when Brindley and Foster moved in.

CHARLES BRINDLEY,
ORGAN BUILDER
CARVER STREET,
SHEFFIELD.

The Instruments by C. B. are CONSTRUCTED THROUGHOUT
upon the most approved plan of

GERMAN
ORGAN BUILDING,

AND ARE FAR

CHEAPER AND BETTER IN MATERIALS
THAN THOSE OF ANY ENGLISH BUILDER.

ESTIMATES & TESTIMONIALS
OF THE HIGHEST CHARACTER,
FORWARDED FREE ON APPLICATION.

Tuning in any part of the Kingdom, by Contract or otherwise.

Colombia Place, taken from Suffolk Road

A new role for Colombia Place

After the file works the building became a brush making business. William Wigfall set up this business in 1868 and it is then that the grand royal crest on the frontage was added.

The new organ building firm on the premises was known as the Suffolk Road Workshops and Brindley and Foster were based there until 1936.

In 1938 Holmes and Youssle Ltd, Automobile Engineers, moved in, staying until 1973 and after them followed various car repairers and dealers.

Colombia Place is still standing today, opposite the Co op funeral services and just past the Midland Railway Station towards Queens Road, on the right.

At the time of writing it is being turned into an accommodation complex of one and two bedroom apartments, set in the heart of the Cultural industries Quarter.

A horse that rides nearby

Cutting own the right hand side of the Abbeydale Cinema House and walking round to Little London Road, it is worth stopping to see the strange tile logo on the frontage of the 1920's Stokes Paint Factory.

JR Stokes founded the company in 1898. He married the daughter of a cutler Sabina Himsworth. A firm of cutlers had this trade and it is though that is the connection.

Mr CJ Stokes, a later member of the same family who still own the firm. was told a fairy story about the horse and rider as a child. He was told it was a man called Mazeppa, who had stolen the gold paint used to paint the blackbird's beak in spring. He had been tied to a horse as his punishment.

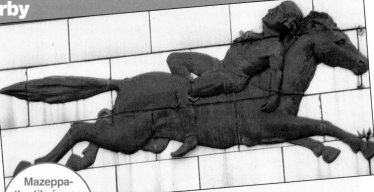

Mazeppa- the tile image on the front of Stokes Paint shop

A fiery Cossack

This story is partly true. It is indeed an image of a man called Mazeppa, who was tied to a horse as a punishment.

Mazeppa was a 'hetman' or military leader of the Cossacks. Born of a noble Polish family, he became a page in the court of the King of Poland. Here he was involved in an affair with Theresia, the young wife of a count, who had the young page lashed to a wild horse, and turned adrift. The horse dropped down dead in the Ukraine, where Mazeppa was released by a Cossack family, who nursed him in their own hut. He became secretary to the hetman, and at the hetman's death of was appointed his successor. Peter I, admired him, and created him Prince of the Ukraine, but in the wars with Sweden Mazeppa deserted to Charles XII., and fought against Russia at Poltova. After the loss of this battle, Mazeppa fled. Some say he died a natural death, and others that he was put to death for treason by the Czar.

This story has inspired many works of art.

The Opera Mazeppa by Tchaikovsky, is based on Pushkin's poem "Poltava" about the events in the life of Mazeppa.

In this opera Mazeppa asks for the hand of Maria, the young daughter of a man called Kochubey. She runs off with Mazeppa after he is refused her hand because she is too young and makes her choose between him and her father.

Kochubey asks Peter the Great fro help but instead Peter prefers to trust and back Mazeppa and has Kochubey turned over to Mazeppa, who puts him in jail and then has him tortured and executed. He has political aims which Maria is innocent of. When Maria learns of her father's fate she goes mad, imagining she can see her fathers blood on her lover's hands and clothes..

An advert for a cutlers firm which uses the same Mazeppa logo

Lord Byron wrote a poem based upon the life of Mazeppa. He makes Mazeppa tell his tale to Charles after the battle of Poltova.

The men are getting ready to settle for the night:

....Among the rest, Mazeppa made
His pillow in an old oak's shade -
Himself as rough, and scarce less old,
The Ukraine's hetman, calm and bold:
But first, outspent with this long course,
The Cossack prince rubbed down his horse,
And made for him a leafy bed.....

Charles asks Mazeppa to tell him why he is such a good horseman and perhaps the tale will help him sleep:

...Quoth Charles -'Old Hetman, wherefore so,
Since thou hast learned the art so well?
Mazeppa said - "Twere long to tell;
And we have many a league to go,
With every now and then a blow,
And ten to one at least the foe,
Before our steeds may graze at ease,
Beyond the swift Borysthenes:
And, sire, your limbs have need of rest,
And I will be the sentinel
Of this your troop.' -'But I request,'
Said Sweden's monarch, 'thou wilt tell
This tale of thine, and I may reap,
Perchance, from this the boon of sleep;....

Mazeppa tells his story, about being tied to the horse:

..."'Bring forth the horse!" - the horse was brought;
In truth, he was a noble steed,
A Tartar of the Ukraine breed,
Who looked as though the speed of thought
Were in his limbs; but he was wild,
Wild as the wild deer, and untaught,
With spur and bridle undefiled -
'Twas but a day he had been caught;
And snorting, with erected mane,
And struggling fiercely, but in vain,
In the full foam of wrath and dread
To me the desert-born was led:
They bound me on, that menial throng,
Upon his back with many a thong;
They loosed him with a sudden lash -
Away! - away! - and on we dash! -
Torrents less rapid and less rash.....

...'Away, away, my steed and I,
Upon the pinions of the wind.
All human dwellings left behind,
We sped like meteors through the sky,
When with its crackling sound the night
Is chequered with the northern light:...

and at the end of his tale it transpires that Charles has missed most of it as it did indeed put him to sleep!:

...Comrades good night!' - The Hetman threw
His length beneath the oak-tree shade,
... And if ye marvel Charles forgot
To thank his tale, he wondered not, -
The king had been an hour asleep.

The Roundhouse

The Roundhouse at Ringinglow

Leaving the city of Sheffield on the Ringinglow Road towards the Peak District, you pass on the right a strangely shaped old building standing guard...

The old building known locally as The Roundhouse is, in fact, octagonal in shape and has been a famous landmark for many a decade.

An old toll house

In the eighteenth and nineteenth centuries, many roads used to have turnpikes. These roads were kept in good condition with the money raised from the tolls or fees charged to use them. There was someone to collect these tolls at the tollbars and building were often put up at these points for the toll bar keeper to use. The Roundhouse is one such building.

It was built for the Barber Fields toll bar, about 1795. It is at the place where the road divides in different directions.

The toll gates are long gone.

Other toll houses

Some more of these old toll house buildings remain in Sheffield itself. One stands at Pitsmoor at the junction of Burngreave and Pitsmoor Road. Hunters Bar had a toll bar, hence the name, but the building is long gone.

Also at bottom of Collegiate Crescent as it meets Ecclesall Road the old toll house is still there on the right, now used as a shop.

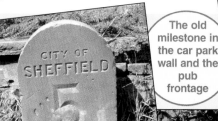

The old milestone in the car park wall and the pub frontage

The Norfolk Arms

Across the road from the Round House is the Norfolk Arms, where turnpike travellers would rest and get refreshments,

This characterful pub with its castle- like frontage is over 200 years old.

There is an old milestone set into the car park wall.

There is also a cute little Victorian post box.

The Sheffield Round Walk passes by here and the inn still refreshes many a weary traveller on wheels or foot.

The Old post box (right)

Roche Abbey

A view up the impressive walls of the abbey ruins

Just outside Maltby are the fine ruins of a once grand Abbey, built in the early Gothic style, and one time home to monks from the Cistercian order...

This old abbey, dating from the 12th century, provides an atmospheric glimpse into of the life and surrounds of a monk, as well as a beautifully romantic ruin for the present day visitor to wander around in..

Beginnings

The abbey was founded in 1147. Cistercian monks from Newminster in Northumberland founded the abbey at Roche. They in turn had been founded by the monks at Fountains Abbey in North Yorkshire.

Two patrons provided funds, men named Richard de Buili and Richard Fitzturgis. They owned the lands either side of the Maltby beck where the abbey was later built, so the monks could choose the best spot.

Like all Cistercian Abbeys, Roche was dedicated to the Virgin Mary.

The original buildings were made of wood and the earliest stone buildings of the abbey date from the 1170s.

Later buildings were constructed on the other side of the stream, including the Abbot's lodging, kitchen and infirmary, and a 13th century arched bridge still spans the Maltby Beck.

The site

The abbey is close to steep magnesian limestone cliffs, which is where the stone to build it came from. The name Roche is Norman French, refering to these rocks.

There is also the Maltby Beck running through the site, a crucial source of water. When the Beck runs through the abbey buildings and courts it is contained in 12th century stone channels. On the higher ground to the south, a stream was dammed to form a lake for keeping fish to feed the abbey community.

The ruins

The main, best preserved part of the site is the abbey church, which dates from around 1180.

Many of the other parts of the abbey are to be seen by the foundations left behind.

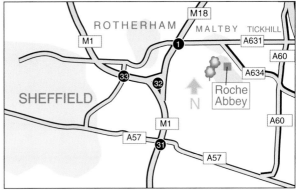

The abbey ruins, a romantic site

Around the site

The Gatehouse

The abbey was once surrounded by a 3metre (10 foot) high stone wall. Access through the wall was via a gatehouse, which led into the outer court. This was near where the car park is now. A lane then led to a second gatehouse.

This gatehouse is the first part of the abbey site seen as you walk from the car park.

The lower storey of this gatehouse, dating from around the year 1200, still remains. Visitors would enter here and be checked before going further.

The gatehouse had a porter's lodge. Much of the medieval floor in the archway still survives. There is also a figure carved near the roof (see right).

The upper storey, now gone, was reached by a spiral staircase, part of which can still be seen. What is left of the upper storey can be seen from a footpath in the woodland above the gatehouse.

In the rocks near the gatehouse are some dwellings once inhabited by hermits, shown in the picture below.

The Outer Court

This part of the site was where the industrial buildings were placed, such as the mill, stables, smithy, tannery and buildings for cattle.

The Inner Court

This led directly to the monastery. It was sited is the area of grass in front of the ticket office.

The Abbey Church

The part of the site most impressive still is the church part of the Abbey, the walls of which stand highest in the ruins.

Here the community assembled each day to say mass.

The nave area of the church was where 'lay brothers' worshiped.

These brothers had taken religious vows but were not monks. They did a lot of the more manual work and attended less services.

The monks used the choir part of the church. The area used by lay brothers and monks was separated by a rood screen, about 4m (12ft) high. This would have had a crucifix on it. Rood is an old word for cross.

In the grass now covering the nave floor can be seen some very worn gravestones.

The transept east walls are the ones from the church still standing almost to their original height.

They both have two arches. They date from the 1170's and are amongst the earliest examples of Gothic architecture in the north of England. They have three storeys and some of the fine decoration in stone survives on the walls. The skeletal remains still convey the grandeur that the church must have had.

One of the transept walls

One of the gravestones in the nave

Some of the ornate stone work still surviving on the abbey church walls

More of the site

The Cloister

When not in church the monks spent most of the time in the cloister. This was a roofed arcade, with pointed arches, surrounding an open square. Traces of the foundations remain and a section has been reconstructed from fallen fragments. The triangular area between the tops of the arches (spandrels) were decorated with trefoil (1) and quatrefoil (2) decorations.

Around the cloister were other buildings for the monks, including a parlour where the monks could have limited conversation, (talking was forbidden except for necessary communication at one period of the day) a chapter house for business and storage rooms for books.

Near the cloister was a warming room. This was the only heated room in the cloister, where a fire burned from All Saints Day (November 1st) to Good Friday only. Remains of the fireplaces an be seen. They are of thin red brick, which are in fact old roof tiles taken and re-used from older Roman buildings.

Red Roman roof tiles reused in the fireplace

An archway on the transept walls

The site in more overgrown times. An engraving from the old Pawson and Brailsford Guide

Also in this area is the refectory (dining room). The monks would usually eat only one meal a day and ate no meat except fish which was eaten on some feast days.

The fish came from their own large fishpond, now called Laughton Pond. They would have eaten in silence, except for readings from the bible.

The kitchen and the monks' accommodation and sleeping quarters (dormitory) are around here too.

Walkways around the cloister had benches where monks could sit and read or meditate.

The monks also had their own infirmary, where the sick and infirm were tended. Aged monks also lived their days out here.

Near the Maltby Beck running through the site was the large day room, where daily work was carried out.

The Latrines (toilet block)

Attached to the day room were the latrines (reredorter). These were over the stream in two storeys. The foundations can be seen on both sides of the river bank. Waste would have dropped straight into the river and been washed away.

Plan of the Abbey ruins

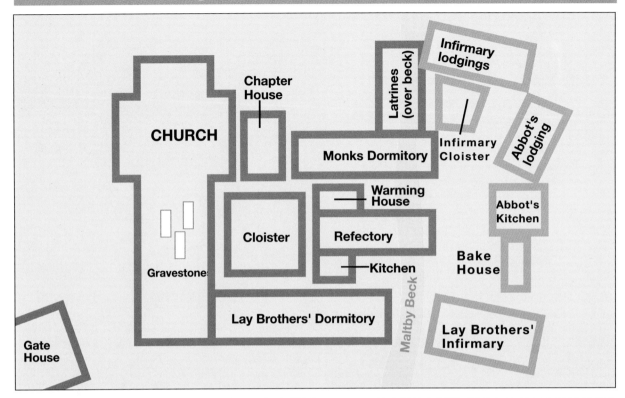

Chapter House

CHURCH

Latrines (over beck)

Infirmary lodgings

Monks Dormitory

Infirmary Cloister

Abbot's lodging

Warming House

Abbot's Kitchen

Cloister

Refectory

Gravestones

Kitchen

Bake House

Maltby Beck

Lay Brothers' Dormitory

Lay Brothers' Infirmary

Gate House

The monks

At the height of it's history, there were around 175 men living at the abbey.

In the late 13th century, the number of lay brothers living at abbeys began to decline. Also the Black Death plague in the mid 14th century killed many, and at Roche all but one lay brother died. The community then had only 15 people, a big change from the 175 in its hey day.

The numbers did grow again over the years, but the end came with the dissolution of the monasteries. This was when the king (Henry VIII) ordered the wealth of the monasteries to be seized and the buildings closed, and usually destroyed.

At Roche, the dissolution took place on 23rd June 1538. 14 monks and four novice monks signed the deed of surrender. It was planned to systematically dismantle the abbey, but this wasn't given a chance as the locals grabbed most of the stone and contents first! Even tiles and paving were prised up and lead melted from the roof.

This is the ticket office and where there are books and information about the abbey on sale

Later times

The site then passed through many private hands, including the Earls of Scarborough. In 1775 the fourth earl did much work on his grounds, Sandbeck Park, in which the abbey stood. Lancelot 'Capability' Brown was employed to landscape the gardens and create a romantic setting for the ruins. Unfortunately he took down some of the ruins to 'improve' the layout and views, notably some of the inner court and some of the cloister and buried other parts under turf and terraces. He also added trees and waterfalls to the site.

A century or so later, some excavations were undertaken which exposed again more walls and graves. A lot of clearance work was also done in the 1920s.

The site is now managed by English Heritage.

There are some lovely walks around the abbey grounds. In May/June the river and lake banks are covered with golden yellow marsh marigolds.

■ **Roche Abbey is open 1 April - 30 Sept, 10am - 6pm daily; 1 - 31 Oct 10am - 5pm daily. There is an entry fee**

The Botanical Gardens

These well loved gardens are a long established part of Sheffield history, and a desirable home to many a squirrel. They look splendid after the restoration work...

For many years these gardens have provided a pleasant place for the people of Sheffield and visitors to the city to stroll, picnic, peruse plants and sunbathe. Many remember visiting the glass pavilions to see the huge plants and the aquarium that was later installed there.

Beginnings

In 1833, a society called the Sheffield Botanical and Horticultural Society was formed. Their aim was to improve health and recreation by building a garden for the people of Sheffield.

The actual building of the Botanical Gardens began its course in 1834, when 18 acres of land was purchased from the Wilson family of Sharrow (who also owned the snuff mill there). The money was raised by selling shares in the project at £20 each and the land cost £3,600.

Robert Marnock, one of the most successful landscape gardeners of the 19th century, who had been a gardener at Bretton Hall, Wakefield, was appointed curator.

A competition was held to lay out the garden design. Marnock won the competition, and designed the grounds in the 'gardenesque' style. This style is where each tree or shrub is given lots of space to best show off form and habitat.

The gardens first opened on June 29, 1836, with tickets to the event costing two shillings each, a lot of money at the time. There was a fete, bands and refreshments. The gardens were initially only open to the public on four 'gala' days each year. The rest of the time they were only open to shareholders and annual subscribers. These people had special tokens (one is shown above).

In 1852 a review still refused to allow a move to admit the 'working class' people at a low entrance fee. By 1898, however, the Gardens had been transferred to the Town Trust and were open freely to any members of the public.

One of the pavilion pillars before restoration

The following year saw introduction of uniformed commissionaires, promenades, concerts and galas, a high spot in the Garden's history.

The Pan statue, cast in bronze in London by Cashmore Bros. in the 1930's. Erected in the rose garden in 1953

The gardens get a makeover

For many years, the gardens fell into a slow decline, with the grand pavilions falling into disrepair.

In recent years, the Gardens have undergone a wonderful restoration programme to give them back their former glory.

Old engraving showing original glass walkways

Plan of gardens

Layout of Botanical Gardens, with a few of the plants you will see there

N

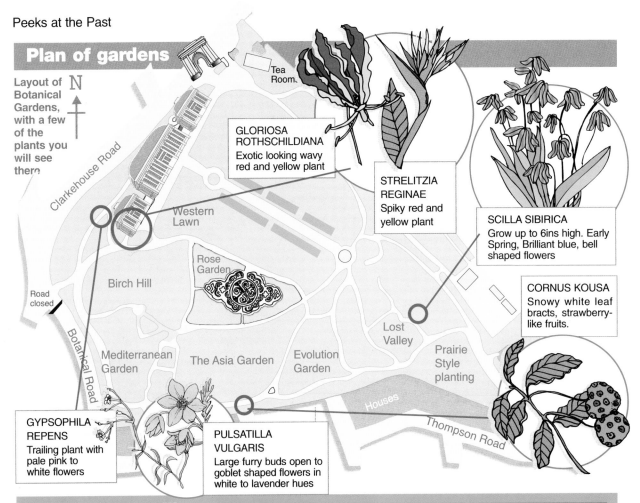

GLORIOSA ROTHSCHILDIANA
Exotic looking wavy red and yellow plant

STRELITZIA REGINAE
Spiky red and yellow plant

SCILLA SIBIRICA
Grow up to 6ins high. Early Spring, Brilliant blue, bell shaped flowers

CORNUS KOUSA
Snowy white leaf bracts, strawberry-like fruits.

Clarkehouse Road

Western Lawn

Rose Garden

Birch Hill

Road closed

Botanical Road

Mediterranean Garden

The Asia Garden

Evolution Garden

Lost Valley

Prairie Style planting

Houses

Thompson Road

Tea Room

GYPSOPHILA REPENS
Trailing plant with pale pink to white flowers

PULSATILLA VULGARIS
Large furry buds open to goblet shaped flowers in white to lavender hues

The Glass Pavilions

The society had also originally held a competition to design glass pavilions for the gardens. Well known garden designer and architect of the time Joseph Paxton was one of the judges. This competition was also won by Robert Marnock, but the pavilions were actually built by architect BB Taylor.

The three existing glass domes were originally joined by glass walkways of a ridge and furrow design (shown in the old print above). These were similar in design to Paxton's glasshouses at Chatsworth.
The central pavilion was originally known as The Palm House. Extensions were added in the 1850's for camelias on the east side and a giant water lily (the Victoria Regia) on the west. These were later demolished, in 1898.

The giant lily was a great attraction and the curator at the time, John Ewing, is said to have sat on a chair on one of the water lily's leaves.

It is thought that the walkways were long gone before World War Two,

when the remaining pavilions were badly damaged by bombs on 12 and 15 December 1940, in the Blitz. They were later repaired in 1957.

In 1960 the palm house was turned into an aviary and the east pavilion was turned into an aquarium in 1963.

The pavilions are Grade II listed and underwent a major restoration in 2002/3 as part of the garden's grand refurbishment. For the restoration, each glazing bar was numbered and taken away for repair, then reassembled section by section. 18,000 hand blown cylinder glass panes were used to reglaze the pavilions.

The original walkways are now rebuilt as before, linking the pavilions into one 90m long glass-house.

Rainwater from the roof is used to irrigate the plants, as in Paxton's designs. It is collected and stored in huge tanks under the promenade. The pavilions are heated electronically, with the central dome at 10°C and the others at 7°C.

The pavilions had a grand reopening at Easter 2003 and contain impressive displays of plant collections from the Mediterranean, South Africa, South America and Australasia.

The pavilions before restoration

Landmarks in the Botanical Gardens

The Gatehouse

Built by local architect BB Taylor in 1834, and made of Derbyshire gritstone.

The design is based on a temple on the Ilyssus River in Athens. One side is used as a shop, the other side an exhibition centre and a curator's office.

The Curator's House

This is shown above in an old print, from sheffield Newspaper archives, complete with curator! It is now a popular tea rooms by day and a restaurant by night,. A conservatory was added to give more room for dining.

The Bear Pit

This used to be the home of two bears until the 1870's. They were kept on a wooden platform with three levels. Legend has it that the bears were banished after a nurse held a child over the railings and it was either dropped or clawed to death by the bears.

It is set to be refurbished and the shady interior used to grow a collection of ferns.

The Rose Garden

This is now in a 50's style layout, but will be restored to the original ornate Victorian scroll type design. Here can be found the popular statue of Pan, complete with rabbits and other wildlife decorating the base.

To the north of the garden is an area known as Birch Hill, which used to have a summerhouse.

The South Lodge

The listed Victorian Lodge at the South end of the Botanical Gardens, formerly a warden's house, is now refurbished and used as tenant accommodation.

The Turnstile

There is a lovely old Victorian turnstile entrance on Botanical Road

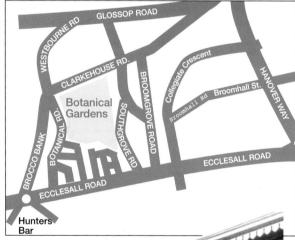

Joseph Paxton (1801-1865)

Paxton left school at 15, running away and gaining a job as a gardener. He was so good at this that by 1826 he was head gardener at Chatsworth House, working for the 6th Duke of Devonshire.

By 1834 he had conducted many experiments into making and heating glasshouses. Without any formal training or qualifications he invented the 'ridge and furrow' roof design, to give more light and also used hollow pillars to double up as drainpipes.

He also built the 'great stove ' which was then the largest glass building in the world.

In 1851, he designed the famous Crystal Palace in London, for which he was knighted. The palace later burned down.

Paxtons orangery design at Chatsworth House

More garden features

The Crimea Monument

This stands in the circular area that once held a fountain. The statue was moved here from Moorhead in the centre of Sheffield in 1961. It was originally on a tall column (see photograph right). The column was broken up and used in a children's playground. The fountain will be replaced in future works and the Crimea Monument will be moved to a new position in the Gardens.

There were lions and cannons around the base when it was at Moorhead. Copies of these lions can be seen in Castle Square in the city centre.

PHOTOGRAPH: From The Star Newspaper archives

The Crimea monument atop its column in the old site at Moorhead.

Note the cannons at the base and the lions around the bottom of the column.

Lion

Cannon

THIS MONUMENT IN MEMORY OF THOSE NATIVES OF SHEFFIELD WHO FELL IN THE WAR IN THE CRIMEA WAS ERECTED BY PUBLIC SUBSCRIPTION

THOMAS BERRY and Co.,
ALE, BEER, PORTER,
AND
INDIA PALE ALE
BREWERS,
ECCLESALL BREWERY, SHEFFIELD,
BREWERS OF BEER FOR EXPORTATION.

T. BERRY & Co., beg to call attention to their very
SUPERIOR SHILLING ALE,
(Brewed expressly for Private Families),
BEERS, BITTER BEER, STOUT & DOUBLE STOUT PORTERS,
Which may be had in Casks from nine gallons and upwards at the following prices, viz. :

			s. d.	
Light Dinner Ale	X	at	1 0	per gal.
Strong Ale	XX	"	1 4	"
Extra Strong Beer	XXX	"	1 6	"
Bitter Beer		"	1 4	"
Porter		"	1 0	"
Stout Porter		"	1 2	"
Double stout Porter		"	1 4	"

Orders sent to the Brewery, or to their Stores, Holywell street, Chesterfield ; or Barnby Gate, Newark, will receive prompt attention.

THOMAS BERRY & Co.,
WINE AND SPIRIT MERCHANTS,
MOORHEAD, SHEFFIELD.
For Quality and Prices not to be excelled.
OPPOSITE THE CRIMEAN MONUMENT.

Right, an old ad from Pawson and Brailsfords guide, for a wine and beer shop, 'opposite the Crimea Monument' at Moorhead.

Right: One of the lions at Castle square today, copies of the ones on the monument

Back to the beginning

PHOTOGRAPH:
From The Star
Newspaper
archives

The pavilions as they used to be, with the old walkways and (right) as they are today, walkways and urns put back

■ **For further information on the Botanical Gardens Restoration Project, contact Cathy Batchelar on 0114 273 6951, or visit the web site at www.sbg.org.uk**

This ancient fossil tree stump is in the Botanical Gardens, next to the present position of the Crimea Monument.
It is in fact a root and stump of a giant club moss.

It grew in the Sheffield area around 3 million years ago in the carboniferous period. This example is said to have come from the area where the Midland Railway Station now stands, having been discovered during the building of the station.

The Florilegium Society

This society was formed in April 2002 and has it's home at the Botanical Gardens.

It's aim is to create a comprehensive collection of drawings and paintings of the plants and flowers there, for the Garden's archives.

The drawings are being done by Botanical Illustrators, whose work showing the plants is clear and scientifically accurate.

This society is only the third of its kind world-wide.

The others are the Chelsea Physic Garden in London and Brooklyn Botanical Gardens.

For information on the society contact The Florilegium Society, Sheffield Botanical Gardens, Clarkehouse Road, Sheffield S10 2LN.

St Cecilia House

IN STOCK

UPWARDS OF 130 PIANO-FORTES AND HARMONIUMS,

By the best Makers in London and Paris, for Sale at the smallest remunerating profit, or for Hire on easy terms of purchase.

WILLIAM STACEY,

91, & 93, WEST STREET,

SHEFFIELD,

Thanks his friends for their liberal and increasing patronage, and respectfully invites inspection of his stock, which includes some of the finest Instruments of the world-renowned makers

BROADWOOD, COLLARD, AND ERARD,

KIRKMAN, HOPKINSON, AND ALLISON AND SONS.

ALL NEW MUSIC AT HALF PRICE SOON AS PUBLISHED.

PIANO-FORTES TUNED, &c.

A local musician named William Turton Stacey once had a music shop at the upper corner of York Street and High Street.

He had moved there from another shop on West Street in 1865. An old add for the West Street shop is shown on the right.

It was he who built St. Cecilia House, the large, grand house which stands near the Botanical Gardens, at the corner of Westbourne Road and Clarkehouse Road.

His initials, WTS and the date 1865 are carved around a plaque of St Cecilia, the patron saint of music. The sculpture was specially made for Mr Stacey by an Italian artist and imported to decorate his new home. The plaque is visible from the road as you stand in front of the pavilions. NB: The house is a private residence. Please respect the privacy of the owner.

Wesley College

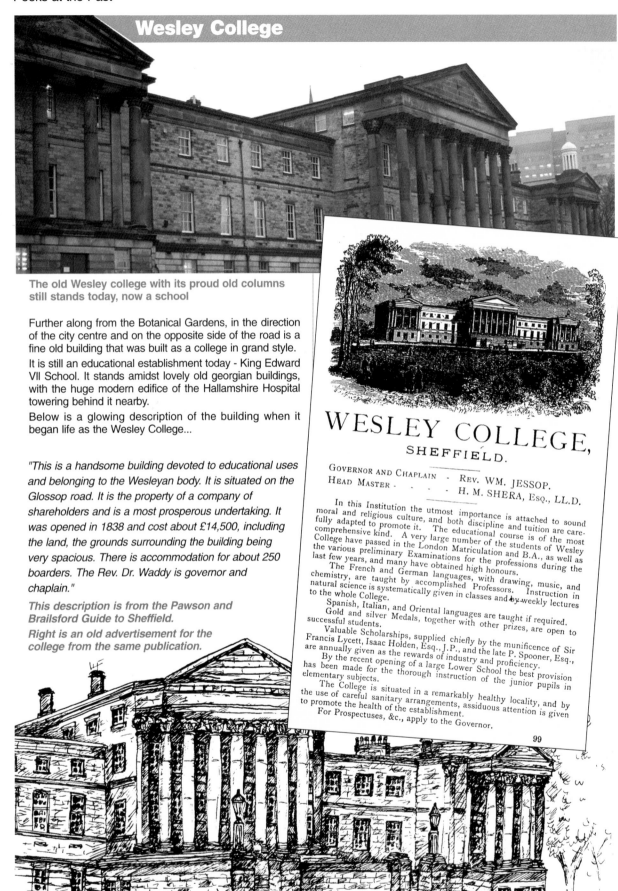

The old Wesley college with its proud old columns still stands today, now a school

Further along from the Botanical Gardens, in the direction of the city centre and on the opposite side of the road is a fine old building that was built as a college in grand style.

It is still an educational establishment today - King Edward VII School. It stands amidst lovely old georgian buildings, with the huge modern edifice of the Hallamshire Hospital towering behind it nearby.

Below is a glowing description of the building when it began life as the Wesley College...

"This is a handsome building devoted to educational uses and belonging to the Wesleyan body. It is situated on the Glossop road. It is the property of a company of shareholders and is a most prosperous undertaking. It was opened in 1838 and cost about £14,500, including the land, the grounds surrounding the building being very spacious. There is accommodation for about 250 boarders. The Rev. Dr. Waddy is governor and chaplain."

This description is from the Pawson and Brailsford Guide to Sheffield.

Right is an old advertisement for the college from the same publication.

WESLEY COLLEGE, SHEFFIELD.

GOVERNOR AND CHAPLAIN - REV. WM. JESSOP.
HEAD MASTER - - - - H. M. SHERA, ESQ., LL.D.

In this Institution the utmost importance is attached to sound moral and religious culture, and both discipline and tuition are carefully adapted to promote it. The educational course is of the most comprehensive kind. A very large number of the students of Wesley College have passed in the London Matriculation and B.A., as well as the various preliminary Examinations for the professions during the last few years, and many have obtained high honours.

The French and German languages, with drawing, music, and chemistry, are taught by accomplished Professors. Instruction in natural science is systematically given in classes and by weekly lectures to the whole College.

Spanish, Italian, and Oriental languages are taught if required. Gold and silver Medals, together with other prizes, are open to successful students.

Valuable Scholarships, supplied chiefly by the munificence of Sir Francis Lycett, Isaac Holden, Esq., J.P., and the late P. Spooner, Esq., are annually given as the rewards of industry and proficiency.

By the recent opening of a large Lower School the best provision has been made for the thorough instruction of the junior pupils in elementary subjects.

The College is situated in a remarkably healthy locality, and by the use of careful sanitary arrangements, assiduous attention is given to promote the health of the establishment.

For Prospectuses, &c., apply to the Governor.

99

George Fletcher

This section is an expansion of the Fletcher story found in Peeks at the Past Vol.1

A name long associated with Sheffied is that of Fletcher's Bakery, with its well known stripey-wrapped loaves.
Founder George Fletcher was a generous employer and a politcal firebrand...

One slogan that most Sheffielder's over 40 will know is the one printed below, popularised in the 1970's as the advertising slogan for Fletcher's bread. It ran for over 20 years and was as familar to many as the loaves themselves.

Betta fetcha Fletcher Loaf...

Early times

George Henry Fletcher was born in Horncastle in 1879. His father was a shoemaker, but george entered the bakery trade at a early age, with a job at a flour windmill in Retford.
This was a hard job. and bakers often had bad feet, because if the hot floors, and worked very early and long hours. They were known as the 'white slaves of england'.
The hours worked at the mill were usually 6am to 6pm, with a break and then another short 45 minute stint later to get things ready for the next day. The pay was very low, about 20 shillings, (about £1 a week) compared to that of a file or razor cutter who got about 33 shillings.

Move to Sheffield

Whilst working at the mill George met and married a woman called Kate, from the slums of Brightside in Sheffield, where she worked as a maid. The couple decided to try and do better, and moved to Sheffield, a boom town at the time, with trades expanding and people moving in and lots of work to be had. Sheffield then was smoky and noisy, but they found a place in the North East side, in Danville Street.
George worked at a firm called Simmerson on Spital Hill. The boss was a pious man but exploited his workers. He is said to have put up a poster saying "The Wages of Sin is Death' to which the witty but bitter bakers added "The wages of a journeyman baker are a bloody sight worse."

Whilst George was working at Simmersons, Queen Victoria visited the city to open the new Town Hall. The bakers were supposed to have a treat of being taken around the streets to see the city's festive decorations as a reward for baking bread and cakes to feed the 50,000 school children that were assembled to meet the Queen in Norfolk park. But the bakers were all so tired they fell asleep on route.

Political leanings

George wanted to improve this hardship. He joined the Baker's Union. Many would not join, as they worked alongside their bosses so they felt intimidated. George also joined the Sheffield Socialist Society and was later instrumental in setting up a Sheffield branch of the Social Democratic Federation (SDF), in Brightside, becoming the secretary. They held meetings at a coffee house in Savile Street.

The 'monolith' - a well known rallying point

Photo from Sheffield Newspaper's Archives

The 'monolith' in the old position outside Sheffield Town Hall

When the SDF had outdoor meetings they often met at the 'monolith'. This was the monument built to commemorate the jubilee of Queen Victoria. It used to stand outside the Town Hall. Many groups and public speakers used it as a kind of 'speakers corner'.Local poet and eccentric Edward Carpenter was also a frequent speaker at the spot.

The 'monolith' today, in the park

In 1905, the monolith was moved to Endcliffe Park, where it still stands, quietly remembering it's part at the centre at many a heated meeting. The lamps that used to decorate each corner have long gone. Now, it is picnickers and children playing that usually haunt it's steps, not fired up speakers.

Out on his own

One of the conditions the union were working towards was a reduction in working hours, to a 60 hour week. Simmerson grudgingly agreed but also cut the bakers' wages. George was so maddened by this move that he left to start up on his own. His bakery was a tiny place at 129 Gower Street, with hardly any facilities. George worked hard to make his bakery a success, selling buckets of hot water for a penny and renting bread tins out, to let people make their own bread in them to be baked in his oven.

Though work was improving all the time, sadness haunted the family, two of their children died, the harsh and unhealthy social conditions likely causes.

Standing for the party

George was selected as SDF candidate for Burngreave. He stated in his manifesto that his aim was "the complete emancipation of our class from the domination of capitalism." he was defeated in the election but still enthusiastic.

A committee formed with the Trades Council, the Labour representation Committee, the Independent Labour Party and the Social Democratic Federation. They joined for a May day demonstration in 1906. Thousands marched from Newhall Road to High Hazels Park. Another meeting was planned for May day 1907, but permission to use the park was refused, as too in 1908. Just after this, on June 1 1908, a protest meeting about not being allowed to use public parks for meetings was held in Endcliffe Park, at the old rallying point, the monolith. A write up in the Sheffield Daily Independent (part of which is shown below) showed a photograph of the huge crowd, with George addressing them. As a result of these speeches George spent a short time in prison.

The British Socialist Party was also founded at the time, and George was a high profile speaker. The Party slogan was "Peace by negotiation." On page 66 of the book about George Fletcher 'Leaven of Life' by Nellie Connole, she tells of special pocket knives that were made to raise funds for the Party. One, the Red Flag pocket knife, said on the box that it was 'sharp enough to cut the throat of the most hard-hearted Capitalist."

A respected boss

Business at the bakery improved and they moved to better premises at Staniforth Road in 1912. During World War 1 the firm survived for the quality of it's bread, refusing to bulk it out with potatoes as some other bakers did. In 1919 there was a baker's strike, which resulted in a minimum wage being set. George, though a master baker, was allowed to stay in the union, a sign of the respect workers had for him.

More meetings

Many more meetings were held. One was reported in the Sheffield Daily Independent, December 2 1920. George made a speech there:

"If a man is denounced as immoral, as a rebel, because he fights injustice, as an enemy of society because he advocates collective ownership of those things which are essential for human life and comfort, then I glory in the fact that I am a rebel."

By April 1923, the firm was known as Fletchers and Son, with son George junior as partner and was at Middlewood Road. They had also acquired a model T Ford car for deliveries. They did very well and doubled the size of their staff in two years. By 1926 they had moved to even better premises at Penistone Road. This factory was the first one in Sheffield to have an automatic bread wrapping machine. Fletchers were known to be good employers, having one of the first works canteens in the 1930s, as well as a non-contributory health scheme. The firm also instituted tea breaks (with free tea) before other firms did.

During the General Strike of 1926, secret strike bulletins were printed by George and other party members. The typewriter used was moved to a different place every night to stop them being discovered. They did get caught though, with some men arrested and the equipment seized. For the trial, George bought them all red roses to wear in their lapels at the trial. Fines were handed out.

During World War 2 the bakery carried on, with it's own fire watchers. The bakers worked through the Blitz, and gave bread to those bombed out of their homes. This was a big thing as flour was rationed to the bakeries too. Fletchers was able to carry on working as their ovens were oilfired, so they were not affected when the gas was cut off. The last move was to premises at Claywheels Lane, a three acre site bought in July 1945.

George Henry died in 1958, but his son George carried on the business. By 1959 they were making a quarter of a million loaves a week as well as confectionery, teacakes etc. They had 40 vans and 260 staff. George Junior died in 1973, but the firm carried on at the Claywheels Lane site.

In 1992, Northern Foods aquired 25% of the Fletchers business and then 100% in 1999. Paul Fletcher, George Henry's grandson was still in charge then, but retired in 2000. Research for this piece was helped by two books - one, 'Leaven of Life' by Nellie Connole, was written in 1961. "Secret Ingredient' was updated in 1998 as 'History in the Baking' to celebrate 75 years of Fletchers. Both were kindly given to me by Paul Fletcher.

THE PEOPLE AND THE PARKS

SOCIALISTS HOLD A FORBIDDEN MEETING,

Tactful Police and an Excited Crowd

THE SOCIALIST MEETING IN ENDCLIFFE PARK

Without the necessary consent of the City Council two Socialists yesterday addressed a meeting in a Sheffield Park and unless the Watch Committee decides not to honour them with cheap martyrdom a prosecution will follow.

The possibility of a collision between the Socialists and the police - a possibility which shrank to an infinite remoteness when one remembered the tact and forbearance with which the guardians of the peace treated the extremists who a week ago demonstrated at High Hazels - was probably the anticipated sensation which brought together in Endcliffe Woods an expectant crowd of many hundreds. Although there was the not uncommon spectacle of a Socialist reproving fellow revolutionaries, it can hardly be said that those who gathered in the city's charming strip of natural woodland for the satisfaction of their love of excitement were amply recompensed for the loss of the usual Sabbath siesta, as far, at any rate, as concerned the sensational and spectacular. Still, tameness of incident was, to some extent, made amends for by the fiery purple patches in the speaking.

The ostensible object of the meeting, which was promised by the Social Democratic Party, was to protest against the City Council's refusal to allow public demonstrations in the parks on Sunday; first the two speakers. Mr George Fletcher, who has unsuccessfully fought a seat in the Council Chamber, and Mr J Maclean, a Glasgow teacher, taxed the patience of their hot and crowded audience by resist-

ing such limits to their speeches as the occasion suggested, their survey of the field of international politics, including severe attacks on constituted authority in a multitude of forms. As a prominent Fabian remarked, an attempt to shoot the rapids of the brook in a Canadian canoe would have been far more picturesque and demonstrative of Red Flag impetuosity.........

"Don't think we have come here to play heroics," said Mr Fletcher; "We have plenty of men ready to come here. I am in the fortunate or unfortunate position of standing and speaking here to-day because I am not going to pay any fine and they can't distrain on my furniture because I haven't got any. Therefore, seeing that I shan't pay a fine and they can't take the furniture, they can only take me and I shan't be much good to them."

The speeches were made in a little dell beyond where the monolith, removed to the Endcliffe Woods from the Town Hall piazza, remains, in leafy seclusion, a pathetic memorial of an inartistic past. Along one bank of the dell runs Rustlings Road, and here a number of policemen - the only police men of the large number of them present condemned to hard work - found constant occupation in preventing people from gathering on the footpath. There were over two thousand people listening at one time....................

38

Around Loxley Valley

This area is a full of history as well as natural beauty, with scattered remains of the water powered industry and memories of the terrible Sheffield Flood of 1864...

Old Pack horse bridge on the River Loxley

The Loxley Valley is perhaps not as well trodden as the other water way walks of Sheffield such as the nearby Rivelin Valley and the Porter valley near Endcliffe Park. But it is just as beautiful, with many reminders of how important it is to the industrial heritage of the city of Sheffield.

A lovely spot to visit

A walk along the River Loxley is a pleasure and an education, with its fern decked stones of long gone mills, and lovely flora and fauna. Many a dipper (right) darts along the way, as well as lots of other birdlife.

The history of the Loxley Valley will forever be entwined with the Great Sheffield Flood of 1864 and there are memories of this throughout the walk.

Starting point

The Supertram and bus are a good way of getting to the area. If you travel by bus change at the Hillsborough Interchange and catch Rural Links bus service 61 or 62. Alight at the Rowell Lane/ Loxley Road junction. Walk down Rowell Lane until you come to the water pumping station on the right. Rowell Bridge is in front of you. The walk finishes at Malin Bridge where you can catch the Supertram back into Sheffield centre. If coming by car, there is a small parking layby just before the bridge, but you will have to come back along the same route to your the car as it is a linear route. Allow at least two hours for the walk. The path on the left is the one to follow and is an 'easy going' one, level and accessible by wheelchair as far as Olive Wheel.

Rowell Wheel

Before taking this path, it is worth a small detour to see the remains of Rowell wheel. Just to the left of the water station grounds. Here there is a reconstructed wooden 'pentrough'. This is a container over a water wheel, which holds the water before letting it drop onto the wheel. A wheel with this type of action is called an 'overshot wheel'. Water still cascades to where the wheel would have been. Cut outs for the long gone axle can be seen on the rock below. Nearby, a little further to the left is where the sluice gates would have been. Grooves in a metal platform give the location. Rowell wheel once had 60 men working there in the steel industry. It was demolished in the 1950s.

Rowell Wheel and one of the grinders there fared badly in the flood

Opposite the remains of Rowell Wheel, on the left and on a path to Stannington is an old pack horse bridge. The keystone of the bridge bears the date 1864/65. This was the date the bridge was rebuilt after the original was destroyed in the Sheffield Flood of 1864. The house next to the bridge, Croft House, was originally the old Rowell Bridge Inn, nicknamed the 'Muck Oyl' by locals. This was in the course of the flood and the Waters family living there had a narrow escape, as the extract from an account of the flood written at the time as the extract from an account of the flood written at the time describes.

Retrace your steps back over the bridge and you can now start the walk proper by following the path down river. As you walk the path, the water on your right is not the river but the 'tail race' or 'tail goyt' for the old Rowell Wheel. This is water passing out after going through the wheel of a mill, to return to the river. The river merges with the goyt a little further along the path.

ROWELL BRIDGE.

The next place in the course of the flood was Rowell Bridge, which is situated at the foot of a steep hill, and where the water seems to have swept along with great fury. The grinding wheel of Messrs. Darwin and Oates was completely swept away, not one stone being left upon another to mark its position. The grinding wheel of Messrs. Elliott and Pitchford shared a similar fate, except one portion, which is left standing in a ruinous condition. About sixty persons were employed at these grinding wheels; all their tools were carried away, and they themselves thrown out of work.

The bridge over the river was completely washed away, the bed of the stream torn up, and large stones were scattered about in the utmost confusion.

AN INDUSTRIOUS GRINDER WASHED AWAY.

At Rowell Bridge Wheel was employed a grinder named William Bradbury, who, being anxious to make a good wage on Saturday night, had stopped behind his companions, and was working all night. The last man, except Bradbury, had left at half-past eleven, only half an hour before the flood came, and another had left at half-past ten. No one saw what became of Bradbury, but he has not since been heard of, and there is no doubt he was carried away by the flood. His body has not been recovered, or at least it has not been identified.

EXTRAORDINARY ESCAPE OF A FAMILY.

At Rowell Bridge is the Inn which takes its name from the place, and which is kept by Mr. John Waters. Part of the building is also used as a flour mill. Mrs. Waters, in the middle of the night, was awoke by the roar of the advancing flood, which, she says, sounded like a clap of thunder. She awoke her husband, and the inmates of the house. The water had burst through the doors and windows, and filled the house up to a considerable height. There was no time to dress, and just as they were, the inmates all escaped through a door which leads from the house to the flour mill, thence they proceeded to a hayloft, and got on to the roof. The buildings being situated at the foot of a steep hill, they easily escaped from the roof to the hill side, ran up the hill, and sought shelter at a neighbour's house. There they dressed themselves, as best they could, got some refreshment, and went back to see what was the condition of their own habitatic

— ..as

Extracts from 'A Complete History of the Great Flood at Sheffield' by Samuel Harrison, published in 1864

Past traces

The first wheel along the path walk is Olive Wheel. A short path to the right leads to the weir and also the 'head goyt' for the Olive Wheel. Scant remains can be seen of the shuttle gate which released water from the river into the head goyt to fill the pond.

Return to the path again.

On the right is a narrow footbridge over the river (shown left). In the early 1800s a bridge here was supported by the original gibbet post from Wadsley Common, on which the body of Francis Fearn was hung in 1772, for the murder of Nathaniel Andrews, a Sheffield watchmaker. This bridge was washed away in the Flood.

Do not cross the bridge but continue on the main path.

Olive Mill Dam is on your left and there is a view of Olive House on the opposite side of the water.

At the end of the Dam is what now remains of Olive Wheel. Prior to the Flood it was a paper mill and after was rebuilt as a rod and sheet rolling mill. It closed in the 1930s.

The wheel, a grade II listed building, is in a semi derelict state. It has rare twin water wheels that would make a popular tourist attraction if they were ever restored.

All that can be seen of Olive Mill with its hidden wheels

The path continues onto an unadopted road. On the left are what is left of some old gardens. The river is still on the right, but now lower down and hidden.

Just up to the left can be seen Wisewood Cemetery and above that is the parallel Loxley Road.

Next is seen a row of cottages on the right. These were built in the mid 1840s and were originally called Cliffe Row.

They survived the flood and were renamed Olive Terrace. Just past these houses, on the right, there used to be two wheels, Cliff Wheel and Low Matlock Wheel. They shared the water from the river. Both wheels were destroyed in the Flood, and unlike Low Matlock, Cliff Wheel was never rebuilt.

Follow the road as it veers to the right. Note the old mill wheel set in the wall on the right. A path leads to the Little Matlock Rolling Mill.

Just before the entrance to the mill, on the left, is a row of cream 1810 cottages. These were originally occupied by mill workers. The cottage at the end of the row was the Mill Managers house. They all survived the flood and were restored. Now they are Grade II listed buildings and are private homes. Please respect the privacy of occupants.

Below these cottages, towards the river, is the old 'counting house' where wages were calculated and given out. This too is now a private house.

Little Matlock Rolling Mills

Just to the right of the counting house is the rolling mill itself. This Grade II listed building was largely rebuilt in 1882. There is a large overshot waterwheel, 18ft 6ins in diameter, which still has its metal pentrough.

The wheel was used until 1957, when it was disconnected. The gear wheels and wheels for the old leather turning belts still remain in place inside the mill. The mill was closed for a period in the late 1990s, but fortunately it has re-opened and is once again being used to roll steel by hand and a new lease of life for the old place has begun.

There is no public access, but the owners are usually sympathetic if you approach them and ask to look around.

You may spot a heron as you walk along

40

More traces

An old mill destroyed after the Sheffield Flood

The wheel at Little Matlock Rolling Mills

Down to the left of the mill is a path that continues over a small bridge and up to the village of Little Matlock and its pub the Robin Hood Inn. People from the mills used to walk up the steep, paved path to the pub for a pint or two. The Robin Hood was originally built in 1804, as an alcohol free refreshment and tea house, by the local vicar, Rev. Thomas Halliday, for ramblers to quench their thirst. A different kind of brew welcomes them now.

The vicar also landscaped the area with grottoes etc, and the area became known as Little Matlock because of its similarity to Matlock in Derbyshire.

In this area once stood an old Cottage. Mr Chapman and his family lived here and were all killed in the 1864 flood. The body of his youngest son was found at Conisbrough, 18 miles away.

Return to the main path that is Low Matlock Lane and pass on the right Green Wheel House, where the owner of Green Wheel Mill lived. There is a dam in the garden from the old mill. Green Mill was an old snuff mill, mentioned as early as 1777.

It survived the flood. By 1907 it still had two wheels, but by the 1930s it was closed and was in ruins. By the 1950s all that remained was the dam and the owner's house.

A little further along on the right is a building that is on the site of Glass Tilt. This was not a place that made glass, but rather was owned by a man called Glass.

The history of Glass Tilt dates back to the 18th century, and' was still in operation in the 1920s.

Almost opposite and on the left are the remains of a rolling mill (shown right), with arched window holes. Two brothers of a family named Kenyon were in business here from about 1912 to 1970.

The premises finally closed about 1985 and the site is left empty and forlorn.

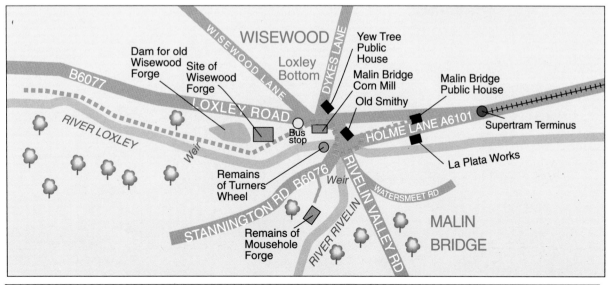

The stones remain

Remains of Loxley Steel works hidden in undergrowth

The walk goes straight ahead along a path through a wooded area. The area walked on was once a mill dam. The stones from the old retaining wall of the dam are on the right, scattered around and overgrown like some ancient Aztec temple. Before the Flood this mill was called the Broadhead Wheel, or Harrison Tilt. After the Flood it was rebuilt as the Loxley Steel Works. This was still operating up to the 1930s. The men working here used to sometimes sit and play musical instruments and were eventually the founding force of the Loxley Silver Band.

Wisewood Forge

Next encountered are the sites of the Wisewood Scythe wheels, or Forge. The dam pond on the left is large and pretty. The path can get rather muddy here.

Water from the pond powered the wheel and then flowed under the firm to feed the lower forge dam.

The forge stretched across the bottom of the pond until just two years ago. Now it is gone, its last wall mysteriously falling down.Now developers are building residential accommodation over it.

An archaeological dig was conducted on the site before the building work commenced. As the dig was in force many parts of the old works could be seen, and old hunks of wood were drawn out of the old mud like mammoth bones.

Debris from the development work at Wisewood. Huge chunks of wood and rusted metal pieces from the old forge works emerge from the mud like ancient bones

The archaeological dig at the forge site

This old Wisewood Forge was damaged in the Flood and claimed a massive £10,000 in damages against the water board, said to responsible for the tragedy.

Wisewood Bottom Forge was next to the top one. It closed in the 1960s. The large dam which was there was often used by one of the overlooking neighbours as a boating lake and was graced by swans. It was filled to create storage space for the Upper Forge.

As you walk along with the new buildings on your left there is an interesting feature on the far river bank - a spongy mini mountain of brown that looks like something from an early Dr Who programme. It is made by deposits from a pit at Stannington that closed around the time of World War 1. The orangey colour of the water is caused by iron oxide deposits in the water, from the mine workings.

Both forges were owned and run by a family named Wood, in the 1870s just after the Flood. In a stone to the right of the path, opposite the metal sluice, is the name Wood carved into an old stone in the wall, but the stone is set in the wall upside down.

Old photographs of the flood aftermath at Wisewood Forge, from the Sheffield Newspaper archives

Malin Bridge

The path now leads out to Loxley Bottom, onto Loxley Road and round to Malin Bridge, a bustling junction after the quiet of the valley. This place was the most devastated area of the Sheffield Flood and there were many lives lost. Bodies from the flood waters were taken to the old Yew Tree Inn, which was on the site of the current one, for identification.

At the side of the busy road is another interesting old mill, the Malin Bridge Corn Mill. This Grade II listed building has a history as far back as the mid 18th century. The frontage of this old mill, with its wooden platform, hasn't changed in decades. The plan mooted at the time of writing is to turn it into flats.

At the left side of the building, also known as German Wilsons mill, is the old wheel, a rare undershot one, in which the water flows under the wheel to turn it.

Opposite the corn mill, across the road, is a stone building that was once a smithy.

A little further up Stannington Road, on the right from the corn mill and behind a dentist's surgery, is where the farm of the Trickett family once was. This family were wiped out in the flood. The farm was destroyed but the outbuildings survived and are still standing. The graves of the family members are at High Bradfield church.

It is at Malin Bridge that the River Loxley joins with the River Rivelin, a fact marked by the name of the nearby Watersmeet Road. Before Rivelin Valley Road with its bridge was built, in the early 1900s, people used to cross the river here on stepping stones. There are remains of another wheel here, called Turner Wheel. This was completely destroyed in the Flood.

The Malin bridge Corn mill, above, and its wheel, below

Below is the old smithy at Malin Bridge

THE DESTRUCTION AT MALIN BRIDGE.

The populous village of Malin Bridge experienced the full fury of the flood, and suffered to an extent which is truly appalling. Within a distance of only a few hundred yards more than twenty houses were destroyed, and no less than one hundred and two lives were sacrificed. Standing near the site of Mr. Trickett's house, and looking down the stream, the spectator beheld such a scene of ruin as has seldom been equalled. A bombardment with the newest and most powerful artillery could hardly have proved so destructive, and could not possibly have been nearly so fatal to human life. The two bridges which here crossed the rivers were completely swept away; the rocks were torn up; whole rows of cottages were demolished; grinding wheels and workshops were destroyed; and the land on which houses stood was transformed into a vast quagmire of mud, interspersed with stones, trees, wrecks of houses, machinery, furniture, barrels, mattresses, and every conceivable article scattered about in the wildest confusion. Here might be seen an iron bedstead, on which had recently reposed some one who had been swept off perhaps while yet asleep. There lies a kitchen dresser, and yonder a broken perambulator, while bits of oil-cloth, and fragments of crockery, tell of the way in which houses have been invaded, and the apparatus of domestic life demolished. Here in

From 'A Complete History of the Great Flood at Sheffield'

The Malin Bridge Inn

Walking along Holme Lane, towards the Malin Bridge Inn (which is on the left), there is an old works called La Plata on the right. This Victorian building is owned by Burgon and Ball, who make sheep shearing scissors which are sent around the world.In the early part of the 20th century they also made cars.

A good final stop is across the road - the aforementioned Malin Bridge Inn. This pub, once known as the Cleakum, was badly damaged in the Sheffield Flood and old photos and engravings of the time show a precarious looking tall chunk of the corner to be all that was left.

The inn was rebuilt and still gives refreshment to the area. Now the pub walls are covered in old photos of the terrible event which is just a memory echoing around the Loxley Valley.

From here it is a short walk to the Malin Bridge Supertram terminus. or to catch a bus back to Rowell Lane.

RUINS OF THE CLEAKUM INN AND ADJOINING HOUSES.

Old records

THE DESTRUCTION OF PROPERTY.

The following is a return showing the number of Buildings and Houses destroyed or injured by the Bursting of the Bradfield Reservoir on the 12th of March. 1864.

	Manufactories, Tilts, &c.			Rolling, Grinding, Corn, and other Mills.			Workshops, Warehouses, Store Rooms, &c.			Drapers', Grocers', and other Saleshops.			Dwelling Houses,			Malt Houses, Breweries. Public and Beer Houses.			Buildings not otherwise described.			Yards of Fence walling.
	Totally destroyed.	Partially do.	Flooded only.	Totally destroyed.	Partially do.	Flooded only.	Totally destroyed.	Partially do.	Flooded only.	Totally destroyed.	Partially do.	Flooded only.	Totally destroyed.	Partially do.	Flooded only.	Totally destroyed.	Partially do.	Flooded only.	Totally destroyed.	Partially do.	Flooded only.	Totally destroyed.
From the Dam to Malin Bridge	9	4				1	2	9		1		1	12	11	8		1			2	4	440
Holm Lane												3	3	7	23	1		2				454
Hillsbro'			1	1	1		3	3		3			1	1					5	9	5	
Hill Bridge	2				6								4	20	164	1	2		7		2	20
Owlerton	1	1							1				1	39	50		5		6	2	1	1000
Penistone Road								1		4			14	6	134				6	4	4	
Hill Foot	2	1			4						1		3	19	68				4	5		
Philadelphia													3	19								
Bacon Island													7	21								
Rutland Road																						

Above is a list of the properties lost in the Sheffield Flood. Many of the mills and buildings listed were in the Loxley Valley and Hillsborough area. The first entry is for the area up to Malin Bridge.

Below is a part of a map in a special free supplement produced by the Sheffield Daily Telegraph on Saturday March 26, 1864, telling of "The course of the Inundation."

Grey Wagtails (right) now flit among the old mill stones

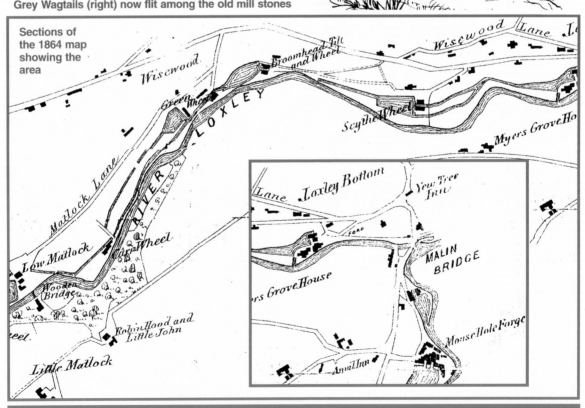

Sections of the 1864 map showing the area

For more information about the area contact Bradfield Parish Archives and Family History Centre, Low Bradfield. Telephone: (0114) 285 1375

Mousehole Forge

The Rivelin Valley was also once a busy industrial powerhouse. This old forge is a lovingly restored relic from those days, now a picturesque ruin and private home...

Just off the main thoroughfare of Malin Bridge, a little path leads from opposite the dental surgery on Stannington Road down to the remains of old Mousehole Forge.

Beginnings

This old industrial site began life as a lead smelting mill. The first mention of any work here dates back to 1628, when records tell of a man called Edward Barber of Wadsley leasing a place in this area to Thomas Revell of Stannington, amongst other properties. Though no exact name is mentioned it is widely held that the place he talks of is the one later known as Mousehole Forge. This name is probably a nick-name, and the site was called Turnholme Stubbing originally.

The site was sold to pay off Barber's debts when he died in 1665 and was purchased by George Bamforth II, joint Lord of the Manor of Owlerton, for about £300. His son later inherited, followed by George Bamforth IV, who left it to his wife Margaret.

During the 18th century, the site continued to develop and was leased by a man named John Cockshutt.

Working Iron

The work done at the site was changed to that of iron working and not lead. The forge carried out the job of refining 'pig' or cast iron into the more useful wrought iron in the form of bars.

Iron ore, natural ironstone, had to be turned first into cast iron to carry out this process. This was done in a blast furnace, such as the one at Rockley, near Thurgoland..

Charcoal fuel and ironstone were put in the furnace at the top of the towerlike structure. Water power was used to operate bellows known as **tuyeres**, which blew air into the furnace to help the process.

The iron melted and went to the bottom of the furnace. Here it was drawn off through a taphole set below the slag which formed on the surface of the molten iron, so all the unwanted slag remained in the furnace for removal at a later time.

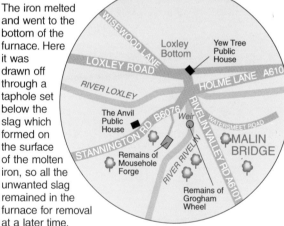

Picturesque remains at the old Mousehole Forge, near Malin Bridge

Developing the work

As the iron melted, some carbon from the charcoal combined with it, therefore cast iron is an alloy of iron and carbon which makes it brittle. It can be melted and put into moulds to make fireplaces, cooking pots etc.

The iron was run off into a series of long, narrow depressions made in sand, where it cooled and solidified.

It is thought that the name 'pig iron' derives from the fact that these depressions running in lines looked like a sow suckling her young.

The cast iron was then heated again in a charcoal fired hearth called a finery. This burnt off the carbon content, making it into wrought iron.

Wrought iron is purer, with no carbon and is easier to work, as it can be hammered or rolled into many products.

New owners

Cockshutt appointed a man called Thomas Street as a manager at the forge. Street managed the place until his death in 1768. (Incidentally, he lived at the farm that was later the dwelling of the Trickett family, which was destroyed in the 1864 flood, when the family were sadly all drowned).

After Street's death, the manager was William Armitage. He bought into the business, which was known as Cockshutt and Armitage. The main work was in producing iron girders.

When William died, George and Charles Armitage took over. Charles died in 1817 and George put an ad in the Sheffield Iris newspaper in 1819 to lease the place to someone else. The ad gives an insight into what was a the site:

...two forges, three anvil shops, engine house and other shops and buildings.."

The engine house mentioned was to house the steam engine used to power the huge hammers if the water level went too low.

George must have changed his mind or had no response as he continued to run the place himself.

A water channel and archway, now full of ferns

An old grindstone stands silently in the foliage

In 1823, George died and left the place to his two sons, Morgan Davies and Henry. Their names, M & H Armitage, became a well known trademark on the anvils which were by then being made at the forge and Mousehole became a name associated with the worlds best anvils. Many were exported, especially to America.

At this time the site was expanded, with more workshops, an office block and anvil store built.

Tools on display on top of an old grindstone

Outbuildings, The nearer one was an anvil store

The famous mousehole anvils

The Mousehole Forge was the first company that made anvils as an industry. Prior to The Mousehole Forge, anvils were made by local smiths, but not as an industry.

Anvils have been made for many special uses ranging from the smallest jewellers anvils to the heaviest industrial anvils.

The old Mousehole Forge over eleven types of anvils, some of which are shown in the diagram below. They were stamped with the famous mouse trademark.

Gretna Green

It is said that the anvil over which wedding ceremonies are conducted in the old smithy at Gretna Green in Scotland is from Mousehole, though this is disputed. There is a Mousehole anvil in one of the wedding chapels though. Gretna Green was where couples eloped to as they could declare themselves married in front of witnesses by Scottish Law, but not in England as this was prohibited there by act of parliament in 1745. Gretna Green was the first stagecoach stop over the Scottish border on the London to Edinburgh run, so people married there. The weddings were done over an anvil, by a 'blacksmith priest'.

The old Mousehole anvil on the right is on display at the forge. It bears the logo shown top right.

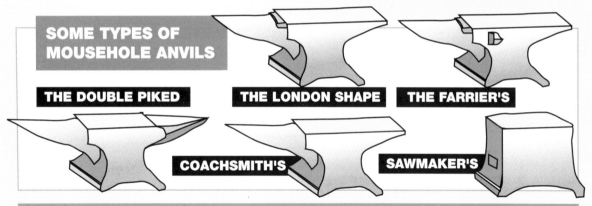

SOME TYPES OF MOUSEHOLE ANVILS

THE DOUBLE PIKED

THE LONDON SHAPE

THE FARRIER'S

COACHSMITH'S

SAWMAKER'S

THE DIFFERENT PARTS OF AN ANVIL

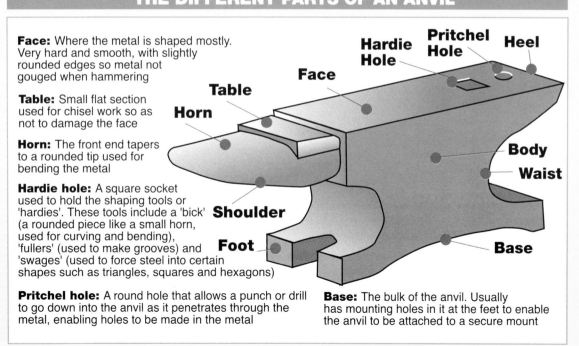

Face: Where the metal is shaped mostly. Very hard and smooth, with slightly rounded edges so metal not gouged when hammering

Table: Small flat section used for chisel work so as not to damage the face

Horn: The front end tapers to a rounded tip used for bending the metal

Hardie hole: A square socket used to hold the shaping tools or 'hardies'. These tools include a 'bick' (a rounded piece like a small horn, used for curving and bending), 'fullers' (used to make grooves) and 'swages' (used to force steel into certain shapes such as triangles, squares and hexagons)

Pritchel hole: A round hole that allows a punch or drill to go down into the anvil as it penetrates through the metal, enabling holes to be made in the metal

Base: The bulk of the anvil. Usually has mounting holes in it at the feet to enable the anvil to be attached to a secure mount

Labels on diagram: Pritchel Hole, Hardie Hole, Heel, Face, Table, Horn, Body, Waist, Shoulder, Foot, Base

Greatness, flood and demise

In 1833, Morgan died. Henry continued to expand Mousehole, and bought the Grogham Wheel just a little further down the river at Malin Bridge. He used this wheel as an extra source of power to produce air for the bellows, which was carried by cast iron pipes into Mousehole Forge.

When Henry died in 1850, he left a widow and six children under 21. The site was managed as an income for the family and was a continuing success.

They produced anvils for display at the Great Exhibition at Crystal Palace in london in 1951 and won a prize there.

The Flood

A tragedy that touched the forge was the flood of 1864. Though the Mousehole and the Grogham wheel were away from the main flood route, they were still damaged. The tail goits at Mousehole were blocked by silt and debris and the site was closed for several weeks.

Also, several workers from the forge lost their lives that night.

Remains of one of the old helve hammers

An extract about Brooks and Cooper from "The American Blacksmith" September 1914

"The present owners, Brooks and Cooper, have run the works for upwards of 38 years , and are still making anvils that are hard to beat either in quality, shape or workmanship.

Although there are now a number of concerns making anvils both in England and America, the Mousehole Forge is unique in several respects.

They were the first to make any attempt at standardizing the shape of the anvils and they operate their forge to this day with no other power than that developed by an old fashioned water wheel.

For well over a century there has been practically no change made at the Mousehole Forge. the same old-fashioned helve hammer, or "metal helve" as it is locally termed is still doing duty and is operated by the already mentioned water wheel.

The building itself, with its old fashioned solid stone walls and low arched windows and doorways, shows but slight signs of the ravages usually worked by time and are apparently good,. barring misfortune, for centuries to come."

The Mousehole Forge passed later, in 1867, to the only surviving son of Henry Armitage, George. Eight years later he died and left it to his wife Annie, who put it up for sale with an ad in the Sheffield and Rotherham Independent on 17th April 1875. By New Years Eve it had been sold to a Mr William Cooper for £8.000.

Cooper went into partnership with a James Brookes, who was already working there. They advertised themselves as the successors to M & H Armitage & Co., so still using the well known trademark name, (see the poster above).

End of an Era

For many years the Water Corporation had been buying up mills to get the water rights and had often tried to persuade the owners of Mousehole Forge to sell. William Cooper's son John later did so, selling the freehold for £5,000, and then leasing it from them at £300 per year.

The forge then was sold to a new company formed to run it, Owen & Thomas & Co. The Mousehole trademark, however,was sold off to a man called Isaac Nash, in Stourbridge. This meant that the new company could no longer use this name and trademark. The name of Mousehole Forge was changed to 'The Old Forge', Malin Bridge.

By now, competition from other makers meant that the old place was not as successful. It eventually went bankrupt and was closed in 1933.

Part of the wheel shaft, now long unused

A much loved home

The forge did not fare well with time. It became ruined and the manager's house on the site was earmarked for demolition in 1935. Luckily this did not happen.

About 1940 the Sheffield Corporation demolished some of the walls as they were unsafe. It was thought maybe the site could be preserved, but the Second World War brought those plans to a halt.

The waterwheels were taken for scrap and the forge buildings were flattened. Some people took stones to re-use them. The dam, once used to skate on in winter, became silted up and the site became a dumping ground for all sorts of rubbish.

In the 1970s, a man leased the anvil store and the manager's house to rear and kill chickens in.

A timely rescue

In 1983, the old forge was rescued by John and Julia Hatfield, who lived not far away at Owlerton.

They had seen the place many times and decided to buy the freehold when they heard it was up for sale.

They first began their mammoth task on Christmas Day 1983, when they set foot on the site as owners.

The work needed was immense. The anvil store and the manager's house were boarded up, The roof and the upper storey of the manager's house had even collapsed altogether. Even so, after much hard work, it was fit to move into by 20th December 1984 and became the family home.

The site needed clearing up next and luckily Volserve, a group of young voluntary workers, helped with this. From April 1987-April 1988 they moved over 1,500 tons of rubble and rubbish- and filled 160 large skips with it. In 1988 the site became a scheduled ancient monument, which reflects its importance in industrial history.

Research

Much information in this chapter is from Julia Hatfield's MA research work on the Mousehole Forge.

She and her husband John have written widely on local history, including a book about Thomas Boulsover, The Oldest Sheffield Plater and information leaflets for the church in High Bradfield.

Their dedication and tireless work restoring and preserving the site have saved this historic place from being lost forever. It is visited by historians and blacksmiths from as far away as the USA and the name is still known worldwide today.

The forge is visible through the gates from the footpath. Remember, that though it is part of the city's heritage, it is a hard won and lovely private home, so please respect the privacy of the owners.

An overview of the Mousehole Forge site

Do you know where they are?

These carvings are in the city centre, except for which No 6, which are near Millhouses Park. See if you can recognise them all, or if you spot them next time you pass them by...

1. Woman's head from the highly decorated Wharncliffe House on Queen Street
2. Whiskered head on Black Swan Walk, just off Fargate
3. Dolphins on domed West Street building, just opposite Glossop Road Baths
4. Vulcan from Hutton's Works on West Street
5. Pig and owl from the Sheffield Cathedral grounds, near the Montgomery statue
6. Parrot and Squirrel on a bank to the left of the Robin Hood pub at millhouses
7. Tiger from Tiger Works on West Street

Steetley Chapel

Hidden just off the motorway on the way to Worksop from Sheffield is a beautiful little chapel, perhaps the richest example of Norman architecture in Derbyshire...

The tiny but perfectly formed Steetley Chapel, near Whitwell

Steetley Chapel was probably built in the last quarter of the 12th century. It is a tiny but exquisite place, with charmingly grotesque carvings adorning its walls.

A tiny gem

This chapel of All Saints at Steetley is roughly 52ft long by 15ft wide and is a rectangular shape, divided into a nave, a chancel and a semi circular 'apse', where lies the altar. The outer walls are built of magnesium limestone, the inner of softer stone.

There perhaps was once a small village around the church, but now any trace is hidden under the surrounding fields. Or maybe it was the private chapel of a rich family who lived nearby. It is said to have been built by a man called Gley de Breton, as his private chapel.

No one really knows why this elaborate building stands where it does. The village of Whitwell is the nearest place, and is this chapel's parish, otherwise the chapel now seems strangely away from it all.

The semi-circular apse of the chapel. Note the floral line of carving half way up, under the bottom of the windows

Saved from the elements

The chapel once had fallen sadly into decay. It was used as a cowshed and was for a long time without a roof, overgrown and open to the elements. A guide available at the chapel shows a drawing of the chapel then. It was rescued in the 1870's by a Victorian architect called J L Pearson. He built a new roof, raising the height by about a foot. He also added the 'pediment' (triangular area) over the main south door entrance. In 1880 the Bishop of lichfield reconsecrated the building.

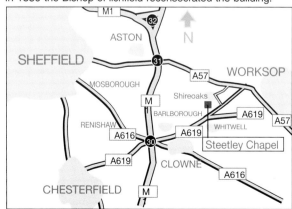

The splendid porch

The main south door has a wonderfully elaborate porch, consisting of arches within arches, standing on pillars and the typically Norman style decoration of zig zags. There are heavily carved support pillars, though much of the lovely carving is weatherworn.

The triangular pediment above is the one added in Victorian times by Pearson. There is a row of larger beaked animal like (zoomorphic) heads under the pediment, like something from the Muppet Show.

The chapel windows are original Norman ones, except for the south side which is later.

The main door porch, with Norman archway and restored pediment. The row of corbel heads under it are shown enlarged below. The ones right are at the right hand side of the porch. The heads continue around the walls

The interior

During the restoration a gravestone was found set across the entrance. It is now placed inside the chapel as you enter and can be seen to be decorated with celtic crosses and symbols of the Mass, including the hand of God blessing bread and a chalice of wine. It is said that this is a monument to Lawrence de Leche, a priest who was at the chapel at the time of the Black Death plague in 1349.

He died seven years later and was buried and was buried in front of the porch as a sign of pety, so that worshippers might tread upon his bones as they went in to pray.

He was said to be a great healer, comforting the sick and dying. This is what earned him the nickname 'Le Leche'. This means 'the leech' a name given to doctors at the time because they often used leeches in blood letting treatments at the time.

Elaborate carvings

There are some wonderful carvings on the capitals (Decorated tops) of the pillars inside the church.

The two pillars at the left of the triple chancel arch show a double bodied lion (on the left) and a cartoonish representation of St George waving a sword and shield (highlighted above right), along with the dragon.

Decoration on the stone of Lawrence de Leche

Looking at the apse through the arches, showing the four ribs supporting the roof. In the centre where the ribs meet is a round medallion carving of a ' lamb of god.'

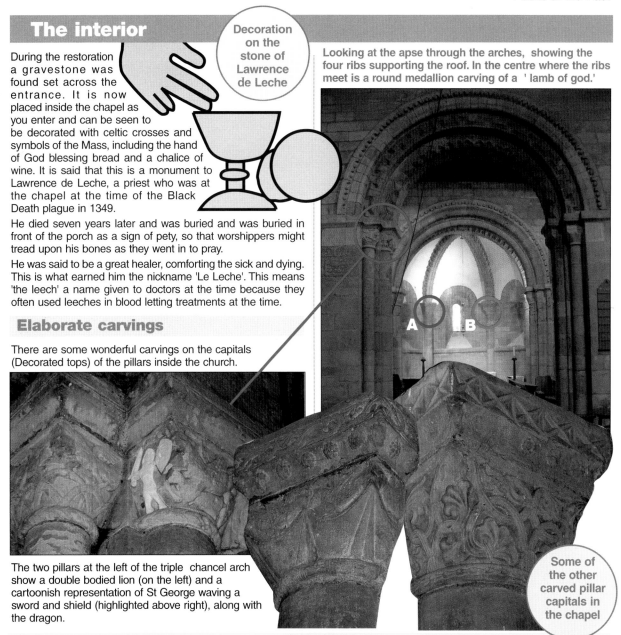

Some of the other carved pillar capitals in the chapel

The apse has carved pillars too. On the left one - **A** in the picture top right is the tree of knowledge in the Garden of Eden, laden with fruit. Round it curls the serpent and on either side stand Adam and Eve, shielding their modesty with large leaves.

The pillar at the right of the apse - **B** in the picture top right shows two doves.

Adam

Eve

The windows

This rainbow shaded window is found in the apse

Chapel sign

This sign is at the left of the road as you are coming along the A69 Sheffield to Worksop Road. The left turn to the chapel is immediately after it and is signed 'Shireoaks and Thorpe.' The chapel is then a little way along on the left. There is a small car park in a field next to it.

GIVEN BY EVA MARIE AND ALFRED THORNTON

TO THE GLORY OF GOD

The stained glass inside the church is modern and abstract, with beautiful colours creating dappled patches of light on the old stone walls. It is dedicated to members of the Thornton family.

The one shown above has within it a perfect little representation of the Steetley chapel apse.

This is highlighted in the circle and shown enlarged in the photograph above right.

The restored pediment and the line of corbel heads

STEETLEY CHAPEL
Church of All Saints

An architectural gem of the Norman Period AD 120

The Man-Monkey

Harvey Teasdale's old school, on Carver Street

One of Sheffield's larger than life characters of the past is a man named Harvey Teasdale, who made his fortune by impersonating a monkey in his stage act...

Harvey Teasdale was born at Sheffield Park in 1817. His father was a spring knife manufacturer and also kept a grocery shop at the top of Broad Lane, opposite St. George's church, but Harvey was destined to follow a very different career.

NATIONAL SCHOOL BUILT BY SUBSCRIPTION 1812

The young clown

Harvey was a pupil at the National School on Carver Street, in Sheffield City Centre. The school is still there, though now turned into a bar. A sign with the school name is also still there, high in the front gable wall, above the old main entrance. The youngster hardly ever went to his lessons, however, as he says in his rather self righteous autobiography 'The Life and Adventures of Harvey Teasdale, the Converted Clown and Man Monkey':

"I seldom went unless my sisters took me. Often, instead of attending to my schooling, I went down to the Wicker Bridge, running up to my neck in the water, with my clothes on, to amuse the blacksmiths who worked st the waterside and who used to give me half-pence for this trick. When it was near the time for school to close, I would run up to Sanderson's furnace wall, in West Street and lean against it till my clothes were dry and then go home as if I had been at school."

After the Carver Street school, he says he was sent to the Netherthorpe Academy, which used to be situated at the top of Hoyle Street. Here he was already showing signs of his future path in the theatre and his later famous role:

"I used to amuse the scholars by leaping through hoops and over chairs like a monkey."

After his schooling, Harvey went to work with his father, as a cutler, but this didn't last long as he kept getting into fights when he was running errands and he decided to travel.

Teasdale could never look at the Cholera Monument near the railway station "without a shudder "at his own narrow escape.

He was lucky enough to survive the disease, which spurred him on with his wish to travel. He and a friend decided to walk to London to chance their fortune.

At the end of the first day's walking they had reached Chesterfield, when it started to rain and the two were cold and sorry for themselves. The big adventure was called off and they headed for home, arriving at three in the morning, wet and tired.

The Cholera monument, sited near Granville Road, as it was in Harvey's time

Just after this, Harvey began his theatrical career in earnest. formed an Amateur Dramatic Society. They performed once a week at the 'Black Brewery' which was on Edward Street, Sheffield. He was nervous of the experience and says this is where he first tried alcohol, which became a blight o his life:

"Once Expecting a crowded house, I took what may seem strange to some, for the first time in my life, a drop of gin. Oh! I remember, how like a thief I stole into Adam's dram shop, in Church Street, to buy the dram and how, still more like a thief, I skulked into St James' Street to drink it."

Harvey in monkey guise, with a duck from one of later escapades

A growing reputation

Next Harvey took his dramatics to The Queen, which stood in Scotland Street near the city centre.

Here he says the scenery they had was much better when they performed a piece called 'The Sea, The Sea and the Ocean Child'. A stormy sea was portrayed by several boys moving under a sheet of painted canvas and thunder by a sheet of metal. Unfortunately the scenery around collapsed and the performance ended in uproar.

The reputation of Harvey Teasdale's performance grew and he was doing well for himself. He even says he was seen at the time as a 'rising star'. He held some shows at "the back of the Brown Cow , Lee Croft" .

Chartists and a broken dream

The Chartist uprising also touched his life: "One night a watchman was shot at by a Chartist near to our house; the shot went through his hat and grazed his head."

The watchman accused Harvey of the shooting as he had a pistol hung on his house wall, but he was let off as the gun was too old to have been capable of use.

Another event in the course of Harvey Teasdale's life is when a clown called Phillips came to Sheffield, to find actors for a travelling theatre. Harvey joined and duly followed the troupe, setting off walking to Retford on a cold winter's morning, dreaming of fame and fortune. Alas for Harvey;

"Instead of embracing, as we had hoped, Dame Fortune dressed in her holiday clothes, we found, as many others have done, that there are two ladies in the fortune family and that instead of the mother we had got the daughter, Mis-fortune, in her most beggarly garb."

Giving up this dream, he made his way back home and ended up working for a while at a theatre in Conisbrough. Next he returned to Sheffield and opened a piece entitled 'The Factory Strike' at The Adelphi Theatre. This theatre had not being doing very well. but Harvey's production played to a full house.

The man-monkey is born

Around this time a man called Milner brought a travelling theatre to the city. Harvey was given the job of clown and invented a new character for his act- that of a monkey.

Their first engagement was in Halifax, so it was there that the public saw for the first time the role that made Harvey Teasdale a celebrity - the acrobatic and daring man-monkey.

A daring publicity stunt

Back at the Adelphi, the fortunes were flagging again.

Harvey decided to stage a stunt that would gain attention and so promote the theatre:

"I advertised, in flaming placards, that I would sail down the river (Don) in a washing tub drawn by ducks."

According to Harvey, 70,000 people turned up to see the spectacle, but an unforseen consequence took place:

"Just as I got opposite Cocker's wire works, the force of the crowd was so strong, that a wall, covered with people, fell into the water. I remember seeing a pair of crutches appear above the water and then going down and an old woman rising....she screamed for help and cursed old Harvey and his ducks."

However, the stunt appears to have worked as that night the Adelphi was full from floor to ceiling. The stunt also merited a newspaper write-up, (see below).

"Thousands of persons, male and female, were attracted together on Monday week to see Mr Harvey Teasdale,a clown connected with the circus in Sheffield, drawn by foru ducks from the Iron Bridge to Lady's Bridge, in the Wicker. All the avenues leading to the river were crammed to excess and the bridges contained many hundreds.....The clown made a start with his tub and ducks from the Iron Bridge; but they were completely unmanageable and he rolled and rocked about with his short paddles till he got a good dousing; but being a good swimmer, he cared little about the ducking.

At this juncture, the scene was changed from merriment to disaster, as about twenty yards off a wall fell in a yard in the Wicker, laden with spectators, including four or five females and nearly thirty were precipitated into the water beneath, a depth of at least ten feet from the yard.

Fortunately, it was not deep enough to drown any of them, but several met with severe bruises and contusions."

This article is from the newspaper cuttings about Teasdale in the Local History Library

Beer and crime

Harvey the publican

Harvey Teasdale also ran a number of public houses, probably not the best occupation for someone with a drink problem.

He had the Norfolk Hotel, which stood then at Barker's Pool, where he sold *"on average, ten barrels of ale, thirty six gallons each, per week."* He also ran a soup kitchen there on thursdays to get publicity. He also ran a pub called the Three Tuns, whilst still managing to perform as the monkey man;

"Many a time have I dressed myself for the night, performed the monkey, come back to the three tuns, played at cards till the next night's performance without changing my dress."

I don't know if this Three Tuns was the one which used to stand on Leopold Street (closed 1987 for the Orchard Square development) or the distinctively shaped one still standing at 39 Silver Street Head (near Paradise Square).

Harvey also mentions in his autobiography that he ran a pub called the The Clown's Head, but doesn't say where it was. He does, however, describe it, saying *"never was there folly so hideously and wickedly portrayed as in the scenes that were nightly acted in that cauldron of insanity, vice and folly."*

In 1852 a there is a reference in the Sheffield Independent to a pub called the Clown and Monkey which stood somewhere in Paradise Square. This states that it was the "resort of thieves, dog fighters and the lowest possible company."

It certainly sounds as though it is the same one that Harvey calls the Clown's Head and ought to have been owned by him!

Silver Street Head and Paradise Square- also places well frequented by Harvey Teasdale and his public houses

The dark side

Harvey also had domestic problems - while he was touring Dublin his wife left him, taking his two daughters with her. He eventually persuaded her to come home with him back to Sheffield and gave up touring for a while, taking a pub at number 3 Silver Street Head,(perhaps the aforementioned Clown and Monkey?)

It was not long before he was off again though, with a group of serenaders. This venture lost him money and he had to play the monkey now and again to make some cash.

His wife left him again and this time refused to return, so, as Harvey says in his autobiography ...

" I bought a pistol, got some drink and sought my wife and urged her to live with me again. She refused. I fired the pistol, happily missed my aim and then tried to take my own life."

He neglects to mention that he tried to cut her throat with a razor too- as mentioned in the trial reports.

He was taken to Wakefield Prison for trial and sentenced to hard labour in gaol for two years.

"HARVEY TEASDALE, 46, indicted for feloniously wounding his wife, Sarah Teasdale, at Sheffield on the 4th August last. Mr Vernon Blackburn prosecuted and Mr Shaw defended the prisoner.

Mr Blackburn, in stating the case, said he could not go into the charge which had been preferred against the prisoner of shooting his wife with a pistol, but would go upon the charge of wounding with a razor, with intent to do grievous bodily harm."

Harvey said:

"The pistol must have gone off while we were scuffling. We use pistols on stage. My intention was to cut my own throat."

"The jury to the surprise of the whole court, found the prisoner guilty of unlawfully wounding....the judge felt it would be his duty to sentence him to the longest term of imprisonment the law allowed, which was that he be kept to hard labour in the gaol for two years."

From the newspaper article of December 13th, 1862, about the court case against Harvey.

Harvey sees the light

It was during his prison sentence that Harvey had an experience that changed his life forever.

He had a vision of the cross and the Lamb of God. So the once drunken clown and monkey became a strict Christian, converted to Methodism and determined to start saving the souls of others as soon as possible.

When he was released, in November 1864, Harvey was determined to be a different character and began preaching to save souls, but many people were dubious of his change of heart.

He joined the Hallelujah Band, which consisted of people who said they had been 'converted from infidelity to religion' and became a successful lay preacher, touring with the band around Primitive Methodist Chapels in different towns and delivering 'the message' in his own unique style.

Death of the monkey

In 1864 Harvey decided to have a public and flamboyant demonstration to break any links with his evil past. He says in his autobiography:

"I had in my possession my clown and monkey dresses, with my other stage properties. It was arranged between the members of the Hallelujah Band and myself that these should be publicly destroyed. So I took the Temperance Hall (now, of course the Sheffield Playhouse)...The monkey dresses etc were burnt upon the stage. It was a blessed time; sixteen persons professed to find peace in believing."

a report in the Sheffield Independent of January 24th, 1865 also tells of the event:

"The business of the evening - it can hardly be called a service - commenced by a hymn sung with extraordinary gusto by the large audience..Prayer by a member of the band followed and upon the chairman announcing an address by another member, great uproar and cries for Harvey followed.After silence was procured the address was given but was listened to very impatiently.At its conclusion, Harvey Teasdale came to the front of the platform...and produced a bag containing his 'properties'. ..The last property to be destroyed was 'the monkey' and the audience were requested not to be frightened though it was "very hideous" . A large stuffed figure was then brought on. It was te monkey dress of Teasdale stuffed with savings "to give the people an idea of Harvey Teasdale as he was" and no sooner was it brought upon the platform than it was seized and literally dragged to pieces by the enthusiastic band, amid great uproar mingled with shouts of Hallelujah!

After this public spectacle, Harvey disappeared from notoriety. he retired to *"a small village called Totley, near Dore"*

He was connected with the Ebeneezer Chapel, Shalesmoor in later life and also became a travelling salesman, with a hand cart and a donkey named Charlie, of whom he says:

"I was told he was about two years old, but I found afterwards that he was nearer thirty. Being of country born and bred and not used to city life, when he got to Sheffield became quite stupified."

At the end of his autobiography Harvey gives an advert for his services, ever looking for a chance to perform, sorry preach, again...

Persons wishing to have the services of H Teasdale to give his Life's Experience' address to 56 Infirmary Road, Sheffield, where 'My Life's story may be had by sending twelve stamps.'

Death of the man

Harvey Teasdale died in June 1904 a the grand age of 86, not bad at all considering what he had put his body through in his earlier years!

He was buried in the General Cemetery, Cemetery Road, somewhere near the offices, though his grave is now covered over and cannot be seen.

An obituary notice appeared in the Telegraph and Star on the 11th June 1904:

DEATH OF A NOTED SHEFFIELD CHARACTER

HARVEY TEASDALE, THE "MAN-MONKEY"

A REMARKABLE CAREER

..The death has just occurred of Harvey Teasdale, who years ago created a great sensation, not only in Sheffield but in other parts of the kingdom, ...as the 'man monkey'. Teasdale was 86 and had for some time lived with his wife at 263 Moorfields, where he kept a small shop for the sale of fishing tackle.

For some time his brain had been affected and a fortnight ago, on the instruction of a medical man, he was removed to the Firvale Workhouse asylum, where he died on Thursday. The funeral will take place today at the General Cemetery at three o'clock.

Many decades later, Harvey Teasdale's exploits became the subject of a musical play called Teasdale's Follies - The Scandalous Confessions of a Man Monkey.

This was written by Christopher Wilkinson and Frank Hatherley, with music by Jeremy Barlow. It was first performed in December 1970 at the Sheffield Playhouse, the very same venue in which Harvey had destroyed his monkey man suit.

The drawing of Harvey a duck at the beginning of the chapter is from a poster advertising a performance of this play by Dronfield Light Opera in the latter part of 2003.

Scotland Street was a familiar haunt for Harvey Teasdale. He says he performed at 'the Queen' . Today a pub called The Queens Hotel still stands. though in a state of neglect

This old Primitive methodist Church, also on Scotland Street, was probably well known by Harvey in his later preaching days - it is now being restored.

Around Harvey's old stamping ground today

A wander around the backstreets off Broad Lane leads to the discovery of many fine old buildings, sadly many are in a sorry state, but some are now re used and have a new lease of live.

The old Saint Vincent's Catholic church, for example, has broken windows and a holed roof, forgotten looking except for the huge carpark which surrounds it. The old seminary for the church a little further up the street opposite the Red House pub, however, is now spruced up as desirable offices. Priests once lived here and there was a chapel at the back. There is a latin inscription at the front and a niche where a statue now lost, once stood.

A scroll at the front of the building bears the date 1878.

St Vincent's Church on Solly Street

Provincial House on Solly Street, once a seminary for Catholic priests, now offices. Above is the empty niche, below is the scroll and date 1878

As you walk these back streets, some overgrown with grass and flowers. look out for the long purple flowers of Buddleia, also called the Butterfly Bush as it attracts them. Also seen are the yellow flowers of ragwort- *please note this is poisonous if eaten.* **The striped caterpillars of the Cinnabar moth can often be spotted on these plants in Summer.**

W. Bradshaw Cutler 17 59

This old plaque is on the wall of what is now the Footprint Tools factory on Hollis Croft

MEADOW STREET

The Queen, site of a Teasdale show, was on this street

The Black Beer Brewery, where Harvey performed, was on this street

SCOTLAND STREET

EDWARD STREET

SOLLY STREET

HOLLIS CROFT

St Vincent's

WEST BAR GREEN

The old Seminary

The Red House public house

The old cutler plaque

BROAD LANE

Green Lane Works

Cornish Place

Cementation Furnace

Globe Works

A view from Solly Street showing some of the places in the next chapter

Around Kelham Island

This place in Sheffield is formed by the River Don on one side and the 'goit' of an old mill on the other. It is now home to a museum celebrating our rich steel heritage

Just off the busy Corporation Street near West Bar in Sheffield, is Alma Street. Tucked away in this area are many proud old factories and standing at their heart is the Kelham Island Museum.

Water on all sides

The site is thought to be where one of the oldest mills in Sheffield once stood, probably in the 12th century, serving the old Sheffield Castle by using a water wheel to grind corn for bread. The name of 'Millsands' nearby serves a reminder of this. Water for the corn mill was diverted into the 'goit' or mill race from the River Don. This created a long, man-made island.

It was on this 'island' in 1637 that the town armourer had his grinding shop. His name was Kellam Homer and it is alleged that it is from him that the place derives it's name, 'Kellam's Wheel' which is on an 'island'.

Mill Race

Man-made island

Weir

River

The wheel pit, which housed the water wheel, can still be seen as you enter the museum.

The Kelham Wheel was a 'breast shot' wheel. This means that the water diverted from the river and coming in from the mill race to turn the wooden paddles on the wheel, hit the wheel in the middle, not at the top (overshot) or bottom (undershot).

In the mid 18th century a silk mill was built nearby. At this time the Kelham wheel was used as a cutlers' grinding wheel.

The two mills were sold off together in 1774, when the owner went bankrupt. The silk mill was turned into a cotton mill.

Street names to remind us of this can be seen near the museum.

An old ad for the Iron Foundry which once stood on the area of land known as Kelham Island

By 1794 a second wheel had been added and the mill became known as the 'Town Mill and Wheel'. A Mr Vickers ran it and employed 38 men.

In 1850 Kelham Island was occupied by a wood turner and a circular sawyer. By 1864 it was again used for flour milling and was called the Britannia Corn Mills, a wheel turned full circle! This flour mill stayed there until 1975. The water wheel was still used to power it up to as recently as the 1930's.

How Kelham Wheel may Have Looked

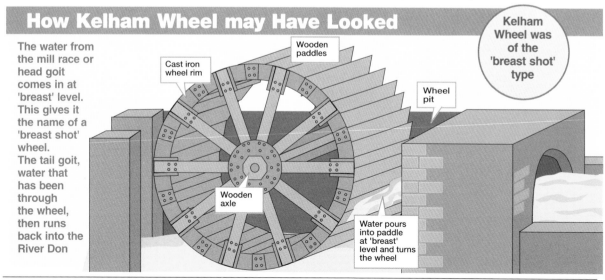

Kelham Wheel was of the 'breast shot' type

The water from the mill race or head goit comes in at 'breast' level. This gives it the name of a 'breast shot' wheel.
The tail goit, water that has been through the wheel, then runs back into the River Don

Wooden paddles

Cast iron wheel rim

Wheel pit

Wooden axle

Water pours into paddle at 'breast' level and turns the wheel

A victim of the flood

Until the early 19th century, the island itself remained as meadowland, until, in 1829, a man called John Crowley built a foundry there to manufacture iron goods.

There were rolling mills and other buildings on the site during the disastrous flood of March 1864, when the Dale Dyke Reservoir near Bradfield burst its banks and many lives were lost. Below and right are two extracts from a special flood commemorative booklet produced at the time, describing the horror of that awful night...

" ...a long narrow strip of land called Kelham Island, its insular formation arising from the river here dividing into two branches. This island is occupied for the most part by large manufactories; but there were also upon it several dwelling houses.

On the upper part of the island, exposed to the full fury of the flood, were the works of Messrs. Wheatman and Smith, saw manufacturers. Here the grinding wheel was destroyed, being battered down by large pieces of timber brought down by the flood. Several large grindstones were swept away...

The Union grinding Wheel, on the island at the time of the flood

There was an enormous accumulation of debris...

Here was a large boiler, there a live pig struggling and wounded; there were trees, beds, mattresses, bags of flour and other articles almost innumerable....

A FIRE IN THE FLOOD, AND NARROW ESCAPES AT KELHAM ISLAND.

Some of the workmen of Messrs. Charles, at the Kelham Rolling Mills, had a very narrow escape. The first alarm was given by a man who had been asleep at the low end of the works. He was awoke by the rushing in of the water, and at once hastened to alarm the other men. They were all congregated together, getting their dinners at midnight instead of mid-day. The first impulse of the men was to run out of the works. Had they done so they would inevitably have been drowned, as the water completely surrounded the premises. Fortunately, however, the gates of the yard were closed, so that egress was impossible. The men, therefore, in their exigency clambered upon the cross beams of the roof. In doing so they by some means set the place on fire, so that there was a flood and a fire upon the same premises at the same time. The flames, however, were soon extinguished by the water, and the damage from fire was very small. A most extraordinary circumstance is related in connection with the man who gave the alarm at these works, and who thus saved the lives of his fellow workmen. He lost his wife, and two children, and his father, who were all drowned in the flood at Malin Bridge. But there is a yet more extraordinary incident to be noticed. His own bedstead, on which his wife had that very night been sleeping, and also other articles of his furniture, were washed

The flood rose to the height of four feet, bringing along with it several dead bodies...Mr Dunn's grinding wheel at the end of Kelham Island was inundated and damaged. The Union Wheel was also covered with mud and debris.

In fact, the whole island was thrown into a state of chaos which can hardly be realised by the imagination."

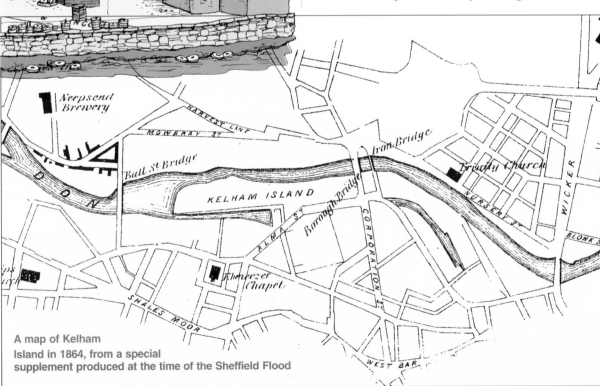

A map of Kelham Island in 1864, from a special supplement produced at the time of the Sheffield Flood

A new use for the Island

The Crowley iron foundry was working until the 1890's, when it was bought by the council and demolished to make a power station to supply the new electric trams.

This began operating in 1899. It is the building that now houses the Kelham Island Museum. he plans for the museum began in 1976 when the Museums Department bought the old electricity depot.

After hard work, the museum was opened on 30th April, 1982, by Dame Margaret Weston DBE, the director of the Science Museum in London, but the idea for such a place had been mooted for many years.

As far back as 1850, a man called William Smith wrote a letter to the Sheffield Independent with his ideas for a museum. People at this time were conscious of heritage and craftsmanship as they were collecting together ideas and artifacts for display at London's Great Exhibition of 1851.

He would be very proud of the museum today.

A view of Kelham Island about 1900, taken from the Ball Street Bridge

During World War Two my father worked in a protected occupation in the steelworks. After shifts he remembers having to join other members for the Home Guard on duty at the electricity station as part of their watch. Many others probably have their own memories of the life of Kelham Island.

The old power station at Kelham Island, a photo from the museum's collection

The River Don Engine

Over the years the museum has gone from strength to strength. One of the main exhibits is the River Don Engine.

This huge and impressive wheel was built by Davy Brothers of Sheffield and installed by Charles Cammell's at their Grimesthorpe Works in 1905. It was used to drive the armour plate rolling mill and was rated at 12,000 horse power.

In 1957 the engine and rolling mill were moved to the River Don works, part of the English Steel Co. There it was used until 1978, and soon after it was brought to the museum.

It was and still is at the museum, run on steam.

The Little Mesters

Another feature at the museum is the 'Little Mesters' workshops, where craftsman can still be seen at work on knives and other products.

The cutlery trade was at the beginnings carried on by individual craftsmen doing a job from start to finish, but as the industry expanded, people tended to specialise in one particular part of the process, eg. grinding.

The different parts of the making were co-ordinated by one person with enough funds to commission and finance the jobs- the **Master Manufacturer**. Sometimes the Master built workshops to rent out to his workers.

The specialised craftsmen doing the work for the Master became known as **Little Mesters (masters).**

They worked in hundreds of little workshops scattered all over the city. Many of these old buildings can be glimpsed behind the modern shops, or have been converted to new use.

The location of Kelham Island

Museum Opening Times:

Open all year from Monday to Thursday from 10am to 4pm. Sunday 11am to 4.45pm. Closed Friday and Saturday.

Telephone: (0114) 2722106

Disabled access to main galleries.

This museum is part of the Sheffield Industrial Museums Trust: **www.simt.co.uk**

A rich industrial trail

On Alma Street, opposite the main entrance leading to Kelham Island Museum, are the Globe Steel Works. Behind this world decorated frontage lies the site of a silk mill erected in 1758.

This first mill burned down and was rebuilt in 1792 as a cotton mill. Nearby street names echo this.

The signage and decorated door arch from the Globe Works, opposite Kelham Island Museum on Alma Street

The cotton mill was damaged by fire in 1829 and was then turned into a workhouse, which was there until 1882.

This was in turn taken over by a firm called Ibbotsons, and named the Globe Steel Works.

Not far away are The Globe works, also built by the same firm This has a grand frontage, now looking out across the busy roadways. It is more like a stately home than a factory.

Above: This sign to a now demolished brewery near the site is on the wall opposite the front of the Globe Works

Left: The owners house and offices at the Globe Works

Green Lane Works

A little further from the museum, on Green Lane, is one of the most attractive frontages. This is to the Green Lane works. The works were founded in 1795 by Henry Hoole and Thomas Nicholson. Nicholson left in 1842, but Hoole kept it on and did very well. The grand entrance archway and clock tower were built in 1860 to celebrate Hoole, becoming Mayor.

There are sculptures on either side of the gate and an ornamental head (above) as a keystone. The sculpture on the left of the arch shows Hephaestus (Vulcan) with the armour of Achilles and the one on the right depicts Athene. Hoole had his name carved on Hephaestus' anvil and Athene's palette.

The firm closed in 1933 and the property was taken over by a firm called Scot, then Tyzack light engineering.

The archway was restored in 1985.

The Ball Street bridge, near Cornish Place, crosses the River Don. At the left side as you approach Cornish Place is a lovely old facade advertisement for a saw works called Becketts.

Cornish Place

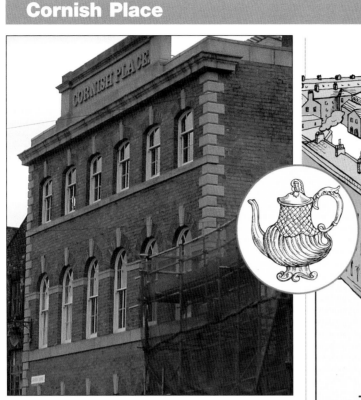

Cornish Place when it was a factory making Britannia metalware

At the corner of Ball street and Green Lane are the old works founded by James Dixon, Cornish Place.

The works were famous for silver and Britannia Metal ware. It was the first of the large scale 'manufactories' in the city for this type of work and was built in 1828. At its height there were over 700 people employed here.

Britannia Metal was invented in the 18th century by Sheffield metalworker James Vickers. It was an alloy of tin, copper and antimony and was like pewter but tougher. It could be highly polished and was known as the 'poor man's silver' as it resembled silver but cost much less. It was used to make tea pots, serving ware etc. It became obsolete around the 1840s when electroplating came into being and was used by the works instead.

Cornish Place now has a very different existence as it has been converted into accommodation for city centre living.

Not far away is the old Wharncliffe Works building and archway.

The Bessemer Converter

The Bessemer Converter outside Kelham Island Museum

At the entrance to Kelham Island Museum stands a huge 'Bessemer Converter' once used for steelmaking. It was last used in 1975 at Workington. The Bessemer Converter was revolutionary in terms of steel production.

Crucible steel was far too labour intensive to be profitable as steel was needed more and more for industry. It was also very high quality which was sometimes too good for general usage.

A new way of making large amounts of lower quality steel at a cheaper rate was needed. Henry Bessemer came up with the answer in 1856.

His 'converter' was a much quicker way of burning the carbon from the raw pig iron by blowing huge gusts of air through it. It used to take days to do this before; Bessemer's process took minutes and did much bigger quanitites.

Bessemer set up the first melting shop using his new process in Sheffield.

John Brown, the steel manufacturer, quickly adapted Bessemer's method for making his steel railway lines.

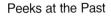

HENRY BESSEMER & CO LIMITED
Manufacturers of Cast Steel
SHEFFIELD.

FORGINGS
In steel of any size.—Quotations given either for Forgings or finished complete.

STEEL CASTINGS,
Applicable in all cases where extra strength and durability are essential, as Hydraulic Cylinders, Mill Gearing, Rolls, Side Cranks, Hammer Taps and Faces, Crossheads, &c. This Steel is of a mild quality and has a tensile strength of from 35 to 40 tons per square inch.

TRADE MARK.

TYRES AND AXLES.

A. The Bessemer Converter is tipped up and melted pig iron is poured in.

B. Oxygen is blown through the holes at the bottom. Carbon monoxide is given off.

C. The Bessemer Converter is tipped up again so the resulting steel can be poured out

PIG IRON

CARBON MONOXIDE

STEEL

AIR (Oxygen)

A description of the Bessemer process from Pawson & Brailsfords 1879 guide to Sheffield:

"The plan is exceedingly simple, but very remarkable in its results. The time required for making bar steel, reckoning from the period when it is put in the furnace till it is cool enough to take out, is from fifteen to twenty days and then three hours and a half more are required to change the bars into cast steel. Looking at these facts, it seems hardly credible that by the Bessemer process crude iron can be changed into steel within thirty minutes.

Yet such is the fact. The vessel in which the steel conversion takes place upon Mr Bessemer's plan is made of strong boiler plate, the interior being preserved with a lining of powdered stone called 'ganister', found in the neighbourhood of the town. The vessel is oval, with an aperture at the top for pouring the metal in and out. At the bottom there are inserted seven tuyeres of fireclay, each having seven holes in it; and through these a blast from the engine enters.

Though the converting vessel is made large enough to hold several tons of metal, it is constructed so that it will readily swing about in any direction required.

In the commencement of the process the vessel is thoroughly heated with coke. A sufficient quantity of pig iron having been melted in an adjoining furnace, the converting vessel is turned on one side and the iron is poured in at the hole in the top already described. The vessel is then put back into its ordinary position, the blast having been turned on to the interior through the holes mentioned in the bottom.

This causes a most powerful combustion to take place. As the fire increases in intensity, it causes a series of miniature explosions of spark and flame which are interesting to watch; while the place is illuminated with a beautiful white light.

The most pleasing part of the process, however, to the visitor, is when the vessel is swung down again, at the close of the operation.

He has to stand on one side, where he is perfectly secure while the molten metal sends forth a torrent of large and brilliant sparks, which dart straight ahead with great force.

When the practiced eye of the workman sees that the metal is ripe for his purpose, the vessel is tilted forward and he puts in a quantity of charcoal pig iron containing a certain proportion of carbon.

The carbon combines with the mass of molten iron and thus it becomes steel.

The vessel is then placed in a position in which the metal will run out and it is poured into a large ladle and thence into the ingot moulds. The process of conversion occupies about 28 minutes."

Cementation furnace

Hidden away just off a busy Sheffield dual carriageway is a brick cone, peeping out from the other buildings. It is a remnant of a revolutionary early steel process...

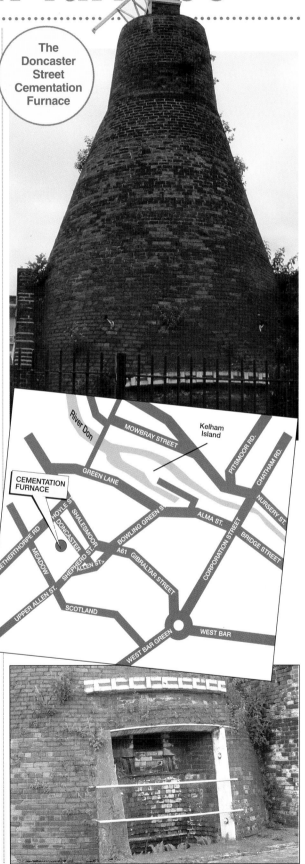

The Doncaster Street Cementation Furnace

A s cars whisk down Netherthorpe Road towards the area around Kelham Island, the drivers may notice in passing the brick cone structure on the right. This is a Cementation (or Conversion) Furnace.

An old industry

The old cone shaped furnace is the most complete surviving example in Sheffield. Once these cone shaped landmarks would have been dotted all over the city's skyline.

The site at Netherthorpe has been continuously occupied by a furnace since a man called Daniel Doncaster built the first one here in 1831 as part of his steel works. The road the furnace stands on today is called Doncaster Street, after him.

The Cementation furnace was used to turn iron into blister steel. This took several days. Iron bars were imported from Sweden, as these were the purest available. The bars were packed between layers of charcoal inside stone chests or coffins that were inside the furnace.

These chests were then sealed on top with a mixture of dust and swarf (metal shavings) a by product from work at grinding works. When the furnace was heated this melted to create the seal. The resulting black crust was called 'crozzle'.

This word locally now means burnt and crinkly, as in 'crozzled bacon.' The word is not used much anywhere else and reflects the local industry. The crozzle resulting from the cementation process was not wasted as it was used for other things, often used to top walls with to make them more weatherproof.

After the coffins were sealed, the door of the furnace was bricked up. A fire heated the contents up, taking around 24 hours to get to full temperature. Any ash fell into the ash pit, below ground level.

An old photo from the Kelham Island museum archives showing the cementation furnace when still in use

The same part of the furnace, now a ruin for ferns to grow upon

A diagram of the furnace

A description of the conversion process from Pawson & Brailsfords 1879 guide to Sheffield:

"The process of converting iron into steel, as pursued in Sheffield, may be thus described;-

The converting furnace is composed of two troughs (about 12 feet long, 3 feet wide and 3 feet deep), one at each side, the place for the fire been between and under them, and the whole being arched over, so that the heat may be kept in and equalized. Bar iron is cut into lengths and placed in layers, with charcoal strewed between each layer, in the two troughs.

When these are full they are covered with sand or loam, which cakes together with the heat of the furnace and excludes the air from the iron and charcoal beneath. All the apertures of the furnace are closed with loose bricks and plastered over with fire-clay.

The troughs usually contain from 8 to 20 tons of iron. A large fire is made in the space left for that purpose between and under the two troughs. It takes from sixty to seventy hours to heat throughout the metal in the troughs.

The process of conversion takes place from this point. The pores of the iron being opened by the excessive heat, the carbon becomes absorbed in it and the iron is transformed into steel; the process takes several days to accomplish after the mass is heated through.

When the metal is sufficiently carbonized it is taken out and the bars are called 'blister steel' from the small raised portions which are left on the surface.

This steel, after rolling, tilting or shearing, is employed for many purposes where a very high degree of polish is not required.

When the bars of steel are put together heated and welded under the tilt or forge hammer they are called ' shear steel'."

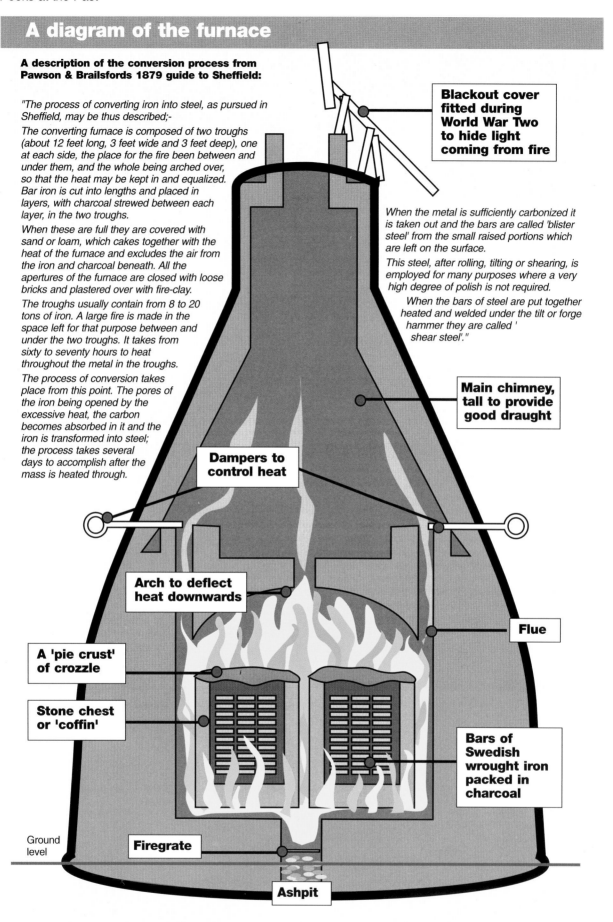

Blackout cover fitted during World War Two to hide light coming from fire

Main chimney, tall to provide good draught

Dampers to control heat

Arch to deflect heat downwards

Flue

A 'pie crust' of crozzle

Stone chest or 'coffin'

Bars of Swedish wrought iron packed in charcoal

Ground level

Firegrate

Ashpit

A fern covered relic

Two doors into the ash pit of the furnace, below ground level. some of the ash is still there from the last firing,

Looking into the furnace, Inside, the arch shaped roof, so shaped to deflect heat back down, can be seen clearly

Temperature was controlled by the metal damping rods sticking from the sides of the furnace, which would open and close the flues as needed.

The contents of the coffins were kept at red heat for several days. During this time carbon fused with the iron to form the blister steel. This was left in the furnace to cool down, then withdrawn to be either forged into shear steel or melted into crucible steel. It was called *blister* steel because of the large bubbles that appeared on its surface during the process.

The furnace at Doncaster Street was last charged and packed and fired in October 1951. It is now on land owned by Sheffield University and in the care of Kelham Island Museum, who hold the key.

Bower Springs

There were two cementation furnaces at Bower Springs, not far away from the Doncaster Street furnace, towards the old industrial heartland near Kelham Island.

There was also a Huntsman's method crucible steel melting shop. They were built around 1828 by a firm called Turton brothers.

To find the area walk along Alma Street and turn left into Spring Street and past the Kelham Island Tavern.

Go along the road and look to the right. Bower Springs is the small street running slightly uphill. The furnace is on the right hand side, now not much more than a broken down wall and a pile of bricks, hidden by undergrowth.

The curve of the furnace defined in the bricks can still be distinguished.

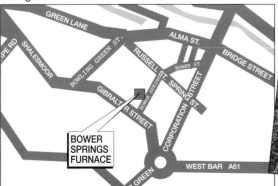

Fire Police Museum

An old building with look out pagoda tower stands just at the West Bar roundabout. It was once a shared police and fire station for the city and now houses a museum...

This old building, once the Police and Fire Station, stands a short distance from the West Bar police station for the city today. It is now home to a museum telling the history of the fire service and has many interesting fire appliances and other kinds of displays.

Early fire cover

In the year 1330 or so, the only fire cover Sheffield had was in the form of leather buckets kept at the Town Hall. In the early 1400s the reservoir at Barkers Pool was used for water, and it was not until 1703 that the first fire engine, operated by hand, was used.

By 1807, the insurance fire brigades were formed. This meant that they would only answer calls to a fire at buildings that had paid them insurance and were displaying the 'fire mark' on the building to show this. Uninsured premises could have the fire put out if they paid a fee. In 1869 the council took over from these insurance fire services.

In 1808 a fire engine was kept at the Town hall, but in 1870 fire engines were moved to a new station near Barkers Pool. More horses for the service were stabled at the old Angel Inn.

In 1876 the first steam powered engine was purchased and as the service grew bigger and better, a new home was sought.

The new station

The station for the police and fire service to share was then built at West bar, and was opened around 1900. At this time the fire engines were pulled by horses.

The splendid new building was a state of the art place at the time, with a fast turnaround of horse fire wagons due to a special lever system.

The look out tower of the station building

This lever system is described in 'The Fire Call' - the newsletter of the fire service - in September 1900:

"The duty man taking the call pulls a lever...this opens the stable doors, releases the horses, rings the bells and switches on the electric lights.
The horse smartly place themselves under the suspended harnesses, a second lever pulls down the collars....a third hitch and the reins are hooked to the bits and away they go in a few seconds."

An old horse-drawn wagon outside West Bar

The exterior

The outside of the old station building has a stone plaque bearing the Sheffield coat of arms of arrows and sheaves of corn and also the city motto. There is some lovely scroll work with lion's heads around the windows. The gates are worth looking at too, as they have ornate key plates with the city's coat of arms on them.

There are also some old lamp holders still in place.

The rear of the building and the elaborate gates

The interior

The fire service moved from here to Rockingham Street in 1929 and in 1965 the police moved just up the road to new premises. The building, derelict, was bought by Yorkshire Fire Service Historical Society in 1980 and the museum opened in 1985, with the place still in an almost in 'as built' condition.

First thing to be seen inside the museum is a rather silent constable sitting at his desk on duty! A small entrance fee is paid at the museum shop and then from here the tour leads to the cobbled courtyard, where the off duty horses were once stabled. At that time it did not have a roof.

The quiet constable on duty at the entrance

Now it is covered over and filled with some fine shiny red fire engines. The nice thing, especially for children, is that visitors are allowed into some of these vehicles. A grate with the letters BP (British Petroleum) is in the floor and is for the underground petrol tank later installed there.

There is next on the tour an engine house with many fine old fire appliances on display, including a Merryweather- the first horse drawn fire engine used in Sheffield, which was purchased by the museum in 1994. A children's play area is also available in the museum.

Some exhibits

The old Merryweather fire appliance, which was pulled by horses

A collection of fire extinguishers are on display

There are displays of uniforms through the years

On the first floor is a collection of period uniforms as well as many other displays, including helmets, medals, photographs and documents. There is also a party room and an audio visual equipped lecture room.

The second floor houses a display of fire extinguishers, breathing apparatus and a model railway, a fire scene and an officer's period bedroom display.

At the top of the stairway can be seen the observation tower, now not open to the public. It stands 25ft above the second floor. Before other buildings were added around the station later, the person on watch was able to see for over two miles. Back on the ground floor are old police cells, a display about the famous old Sheffield criminal Charlie Peace, and a cafe.

The fireman's pole, seen near the entrance, was moved here from the Division Street fire Station when it closed. It was the longest drop in the country.

The old West Bar Fire and Police Station is now a Grade II listed building.

An old fire mark

PROTECTION

1 5 3 7 1

The cells and surrounds

The corridor with the police cells and sparse a cell interior

Old lettering

Up the right hand side of the fire museum, on the next street and opposite the car park, there is a run down old building full of character that is worth a look before you leave. It is covered in old signage, raised letters in the plasterwork.

Opening times

The museum is open every Sunday and bank Holiday Monday between 11am and 5pm. Last entry 4.15.

There is a small entrance fee. Children under 3 get free entry. Open to schools at other times by appointment. Contact:

The Fire Museum, Peter House, 101-109 West Bar Sheffield S3 8PT

Telephone/ fax: 0114 249 1999, Mon - Fri 9am - 4.30pm

Most buses into the city centre take you to within walking distance. If catching a Supertram, the Cathedral stop is the nearest .

Division Street Station

The fire station on Division Street, which opened in 1929, is now a bar. The foundation stone bearing the date 1928 can still be seen on the right side front of the building, almost at street level.

One of the names on it is that of Sillitoe, a police officer who was involved in the round up of the Mooney gang.

The fire service later moved to its new home on Wellington Street, not too far away from this one and continues its wonderful job of protecting our City.

Fanshawe Gate Hall

This picturesque old hall has the most wonderful garden...

The old hall in the picture book garden

Just past the village of Holmesfield, as you travel from Sheffield towards Owler Bar, is a turning off to the right which leads down to this timeless and lovely old family home.

Origins

Fanshawe Gate Hall was owned by the Fanshawe Family from 1260 until 1944. The people who live there now, John and Cynthia Ramsden, have been there since 1959, and are only the fourth owners in over 700 years.

They have spent much time and love restoring the house and gardens and it is a wonderful home full of character.

Although Fanshawe Gate Hall dates back to the 13th century, the architecture of the present house is predominantly 16th century. It was once much larger, but was reduced in size in 1634. There is a tithe barn and this is now being restored, along with the rest of the property .

Over the past decade or so, the garden has been substantially redesigned in the style of the Tudor era, as this was the century when the Fanshawe family was at the height of its influence.

The wrought iron gates, with the Fanshawe coat of arms

The Fanshawe family

Henry Fanshawe is one of the more famous members of the family. He became 'Remembrancer of the Exchequer' to Queen Elizabeth 1st in 1566. He was the first of nine members of the Fanshawe family to hold this post.

The name of Henry Fanshawe is also remembered in the name of a school in Dronfield, which was founded under his will.

One of the better documented members of the family is Lady Ann Fanshawe. She married her second cousin Richard Fanshawe in 1644, during the English Civil War. He was an official in the court of King Charles 1st.

Ann wrote memoirs in her later life, to give to her only surviving son and these provide a first hand account of the war and the imprisonment and execution of King Charles.

She also tells of how her mother was born at Fanshawe Gate Hall, the youngest daughter of Robert Fanshawe, who had the grand total of 12 sons and two daughters. (The Ramsden family consists of a more modest five children!)

The Fanshawe coat of arms has been incorporated into the wind vane and the wrought iron entrance gates.

The garden

The dovecote

There is a lovely old 16th century dovecote in the garden, which was restored by one of the Ramsden's sons and a neighbour. It is made of the same Derbyshire sandstone as the 16th century hall.

It has won an award from the Council for the Protection of Rural England.

It is now home once again to doves, beautiful white ones that can be seen sitting there or on the other rooves, adding grace to the garden.

The old dovecote (right) and waterfall (left)

The same stone is seen in the retaining walls of the courtyard and in the walled garden. The other boundaries are traditional Derbyshire drystone walls.

The ties with the farming past can be seen in the mushroom-shaped staddle stones. These would have been used to support corn before threshing to stop it getting wet or eaten by rats. Now they make interesting features hidden in the undergrowth.

There are also several millstones to be found discarded in the garden. These are now made into features, planted with hostas and alpines.

Clipped yews and topiary decorate the garden and there is also a knot garden, planted in two varieties of box

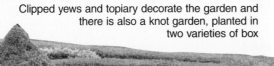

The waterfall

The Ramsden's son constructed the waterfall in the courtyard.

This has lovely stonework in the form of terraced shelves and also a lions head water spout. The water cascades down from the orchard to the courtyard into a plant filled pool.

The plants

Many of the plants have been chosen because they would have been well known 400 years ago and could well have been part of the original planting.

The east facing borders on either side of the entrance to the house contain Aconitum, Digitalis, Alcea rosea, Achillea, Malva, Lychnis, Dianthus, Artemisia, Origanum, Salvia, Lathyrus.

The upper walled garden has herbaceous, variegated and fern planting, terracing and lawns.

A characterful old door at the hall

Around the lion head fountain are moisture loving plants, including Sambucus racemosa 'Sutherland Gold', Cornus alba Spaethii', Iris ensata, Iris pallida 'Variegata', Persicaria virginiana 'Painter's Palette', Rodgersia pinnata. 'Elegans', Primula bulleyana and hostas.

Other plants complement the period of the house, often found in a traditional cottage garden. The south facing borders in front of the house and the borders of the main lawn include:

Rosa species, Lythrum, Lilium, Peaonia, Delphinium, Viola, Papaver, Phlox, Geranium, Campanula, Lupinus, Lunaria, Eryngium, Filipendula and Geum

In the walled "Elizabethan" garden is a 'nuttery'. A different variety of nut tree is, or will be, planted for each of the Ramsden's grandchildren.

Visiting the hall today

Ongoing work

The old orchard at Fanshawe Gate Hall is under restoration, and the new design features a natural wildlife pond and a terraced landscape based upon a medieval tiltyard layout. The trees are local, old varieties of fruit.

The old 'bowl' shape of the pond is reputed to be part of an old moat for the hall and so is very appropriate.

Many ponds and wetland have disappeared in the countryside due to land reclamation and agriculture and the pond will be a valuable wildlife resource.

Water is supplied to the pond in two ways. One way is from a gravity fed 800 gallon storage tank in the field opposite the entrance of the hall. The other way is for dry periods, when a pumped supply boosts the water feed. The water is pumped from an old 65 ft deep well, via a trough and a culvert and so into the pond as a stream.

Plants in or near the pond will include Water Crowfoot, Water Violet, Bog Bean, kingcup and Flag Iris as well as many others.

Plants near the pond will include Monkshood, Yarrow, Angelica, Meadowsweet and Purple Loosestrife.

Pond and Water Crowfoot

A welcoming and quirky summerhouse in the garden. This dates from about 1901 and once had a thatched roof.

Open Days

Open days at Fanshawe Gate Hall are one of the the highlights of the garden viewing year for many visitors.

The garden is open several times during the year and well worth a visit.There is a small entrance fee. Any money made is given to local charities or projects. There are refreshments usually available at the open days, with tea, coffee, cream teas and delicious cakes and Ploughman's lunches to tempt.

There is also a plant stall selling plants raised from their own cuttings and seeds.

Decoration on the gatepost

To find out when the garden is open, look in the local press or look out for leaflets. Alternatively, look at the hall's website at **www.fgh.org.uk**

To get to Fanshawe Gate Hall, follow the B6054 leaving the village of Holmesfield heading towards Owler Bar. Take the first right turn after the Robin Hood Pub.Go down the lane and for parking, turn left into the old stackyard 100 yards after the main entrance.

The garden is usually open from 11am to 5pm.

A book about the garden

A personal account of how the garden at Fanshawe Gate Hall has been developed over the last decades was written by Cynthia Ramsden. Entitled "A Garden in my Life", it raised more than £8,000 for two cancer charities.

At the time of writing, the book has sold out, but more may be printed in the future.

Cynthia Ramsden's book about the hall and it's garden

Handsworth Church

The spire of St Mary's church, Handsworth

In Handsworth is an ancient church that has an interesting graveyard. also nearby are another kind of spirits - at the public house that looks over the old gravestones..

The old church of St Mary at Handsworth is a fine old building that has as its closest neighbour the Cross Keys public house, which was once the church school.

The old village

The name Handsworth is from an Anglo saxon name meaning 'the lands enclosed around Hands farmhouse'

Under Norman rule the small hamlet prospered and is mentioned in Domesday book survey which was compiled by Normans, by the order of William the Conqueror. In this book the village name is written as ' Handeswrde'.

The village became part of the city of Sheffield around1921.

St Mary's Church

Founded in 1170, the church was founded by a member of the Lovetot family.

The tower dates from around 1180 and is of a Norman Transitional style. The spire was added later.

In the 1220's St Katherine' of Alexandria's Chapel was added. It was probably built for Maud de Lovetot to pray for the souls of her husband Gerard de Furnival and her son Thomas, who died on crusades to the holy land. A chantry priest was appointed in the chapel until the 16th century.

A church bell was given in 1590 by George Talbot, the 6th Earl of Shrewsbury, who is buried in the Shrewsbury chapel at Sheffield Cathedral. More bells were added later.

In 1698 the spire was destroyed by lightning. A new steeple was built but it was smaller and squatter and so was nicknamed the 'Handsworth Stump'.

This was replaced in the 1820's by another tower- also struck by lightning in 1978.

Much of the church was rebuilt in the early 1800s and also restored in 1934.

SHEFFIELD PARKWAY A57

HANDSWORTH PARK RD

RICHMON PARK RD

Cross Keys

St Mary's Church

RICHMOND RD

HANDSWORTH

Two carved heads form inside the church

Grotesque heads

On the exterior of the church are to be found some grotesque carvings and gargoyles (decorated spouts to carry rainwater from the roof). The two heads below are on the side of the church nearest the Cross Keys.

This gargoyle is on the tower

The Graveyard

The graveyard at St Mary's is a lovely one, with many old stones to admire. Amongst them are two chest tombs for the Jeffcock family, tucked away in the undergrowth at the back of the church. William Jeffcock was churchwarden 1827-29 and also the first Mayor of Sheffield. There is also a trefoil arched doorway which is very attractive.

There are three stones carved with skull and cross bones in the graveyard

A Jeffcock tomb (above) and the elegant war memorial by the churchyard entrance (below)

An hour glass of hearts and a winged cherub's head

HERE LYETH TE
... OF EDWARD TE
S.. OF GEORGE RAGG
WHO DEPARTED THIS LIFE
... 23 DAY OF SEP 1728
... ONE YEAR ...

Some of the gravestones are very old. This is perhaps the most decorative stone in the church yard, with an unusual hourglass carved on the rear. It is dated from 1723

Inside the church

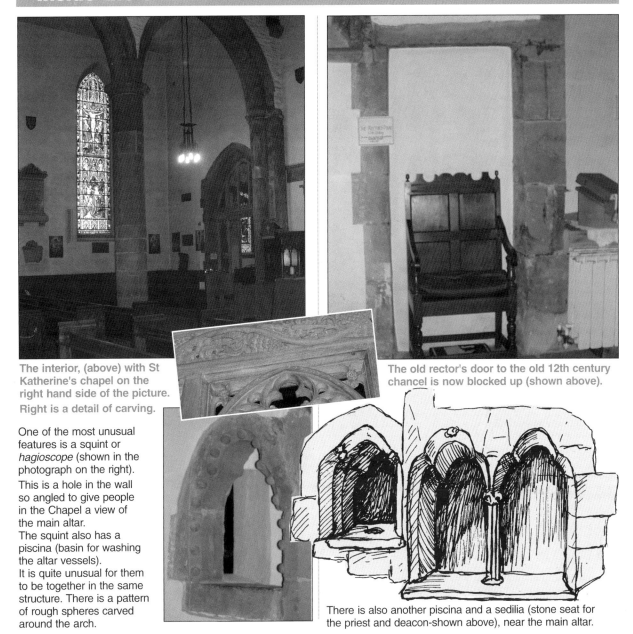

The interior, (above) with St Katherine's chapel on the right hand side of the picture.
Right is a detail of carving.

One of the most unusual features is a squint or *hagioscope* (shown in the photograph on the right).
This is a hole in the wall so angled to give people in the Chapel a view of the main altar.
The squint also has a piscina (basin for washing the altar vessels).
It is quite unusual for them to be together in the same structure. There is a pattern of rough spheres carved around the arch.

The old rector's door to the old 12th century chancel is now blocked up (shown above).

There is also another piscina and a sedilia (stone seat for the priest and deacon-shown above), near the main altar.

St Marys Parish Centre, which has a small museum, has open days. Ring. 269 2537 or 269243 for times etc.

Services

SUNDAY

| 10am | Parish Eucharist |
| 11.30am | All age worship (1st sunday of month) |

WEEKDAYS

9.30am	Holy Eucharist (wed)
7pm	Celtic Mass (Thurs)
12 noon	Holy Eucharist (Fri)

RECTOR
Rev. Ian Hollin

Telephone 2692403

Some of the the windows

There are some fine old windows to see in the church.
The window on the right has a plaque which is inscribed:

To the memory of William Henry Jeffcock of High Hazels, who died 2nd August 1863 and Susanna his wife. Dedicated by their four children

This window is in memory of a Mr John Craven, who died in December18 92 and also for Sarah Ellen his wife who died in December 1873.
It is given by their children

This window is for the Ball family

The Cross Keys

This pub is unusual in that it is bordered on three sides by the graveyard of the church. This is because the buildings making up this pub originally belonged to the adjoining church and were once the accommodation for the clergy and also later a schoolhouse. Timber beams in the oldest of the three sections which form the pub today have been dated to the16th century. A parish clerk bought the buildings in 1800 and later around the 1820s it was turned into an alehouse. The tap room is the oldest part of the building.

There is a tunnel in the cellar of the pub, now blocked, but said to link up to the cellars of the old Handsworth Hall. The tunnel is said to be haunted by a ghostly grey lady, possibly a murdered maid of Mary Queen of Scots, using the tunnel to sneak messages to the captive Queen, who could well have stayed at the old hall at some point, seeing as she seemed to get to most of Sheffield's historical buildings at some point in her stay!.

A central bar serves the Lounge, Snug and Tap rooms of the pub. The tap room is the oldest part, and has timber benched seating. On the snug walls are pictures of the Handsworth Sword Dancers (see next page).

The Cross keys is at 400 Handsworth Rd, Sheffield S13 9BZ. Telephone 0114 254 1050. Opening hours are Mon - Sat: 12 noon - 11pm, Sun: 12 noon - 10.30pm

A little further along the main Handsworth Road to the right hand side of the church is a disused memorial fountain and water trough to William Jeffcock. He was born in 1800 in Handsworth and as mentioned, was the first Mayor of Sheffield, in 1843. The Jeffcock family lived for many years at nearby High Hazels.

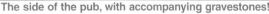

The side of the pub, with accompanying gravestones!

The Jeffcock fountain and water trough, now disused

Handsworth Sword Dancers

On Boxing Day each year Handsworth Sword Dancers celebrate the time around the Winter Solstice, performing at Woodhouse cross, 11.15am, and the parish church 12 noon.

Using long steel 'swords' (flat blades with rounded ends) a team of eight perform the dance, the climax of which is when the swords are entwined in a star shaped pattern, called a 'lock.

The music is made up of various well known tunes such as British Grenadiers and Bobby Shafto.

The costume of the dancers is similar to an 1825 Light Dragoons uniform. There used to be two clowns in the earlier years of the dance, shown in old photos of the team.

The dance has an unbroken history. During both wars, the team remained active due to exempted occupations in the coalmines and steelworks.

A man called Cecil Sharp notated the dance based on visits made in 1913. He and the English Folk Dance Society brought the tradition to wider notice.

Many villages in the north of England used to have their own traditional sword dances. The ones that still survive are of one of two types- either using the longswords or the shorter flexible 'rapper' swords, which have a handle at each end. It is mostly longsword in Yorkshire, with rapper types being further North.

The Sword Dancers in action

The village of Grenoside also has a sword dancing tradition on Boxing Day.

Their costume is of Paisley tunics. The captain (leader) wears an animal skin hat. The swords are made into a lock during the dance, as with the Handsworth dance.

In these photographs, the dancers are on grass which is highly unusual. they usually perform on a hard surface to gain maximum effect from the 'stamping' steps.

Joyce R. Himsworth

One of Sheffield's top craftswomen of the early and mid 20th century was Joyce Rosemary Himsworth, silver and goldsmith, who produced many beautiful pieces...

Joyce at work in the attic of her home

Joyce was born into an old, established Sheffield family, at Machon Bank, on 19th August, 1905. Her father, Joseph, was also a well known craftsman/artist and her mother, Dora, was a schoolteacher.

Inherited skills

Joseph Beeston Himsworth, Joyce's father, worked as a cutler and also was an author of books about the trade, including 'The Story of Cutlery'.

He had encouraged his daughter's talents from an early age - she made her first spoon at the age of five!.

Joyce was also well tutored in arts and crafts at Sheffield High School, then went on to train at Sheffield College of Art. She specialised there in "gold and silversmithing, inlay, niello-work and allied processes."

Joyce then moved to the Central School of Arts and Crafts in London, afterwards returning to Sheffield to work. She gained a City and Guilds of London 1st Class Technological certificate and also a first place in the country in enamelling.

Her father was a partner in the firm B Worth and Sons and Joyce did work for the company.

On her letterhead, Joyce lists her specialities as 'church and domestic silverware, presidential badges, christening gifts and spoons'.

Joyce was a lifelong, committed vegetarian, and was very proud of the fact.

Awards

She earned various awards, including a first prize in national competitions at the Worshipful Company of Goldsmiths, London, in 1937 and 1938, and a prize in a competition run by the Worshipful Company of Armourers and Braziers. She also was given various awards from the Sheffield Silver Trades for both design and workmanship.

Joyce also spent some time as a lecturer at Sheffield Trades Technical Society, Rotherham School of Art and the Chesterfield School of Art.

Exhibitions

Joyce exhibited her work far and wide to much acclaim and was a member of several crafts guilds and societies.

At the Red Rose Guild of Craftsmen exhibition at the Whitworth Art Gallery, Manchester, in 1951, she showed over fifteen pieces of work. These included a pair of silver sardine servers for £7.10s 0d (£7.50p), a silver christening mug for £13.6s.8d (£13.34p) and a swan napkin ring for £2.18s.4d (£2.91p).

She also took part in an exhibition of 'The Work of The Modern Designer-Craftsmen', arranged by the Crafts Centre of Great Britain for the Arts Council, in 1955.

Her work was also popular in other countries and she exhibited in the USA, Canada, Australia and on the Continent.

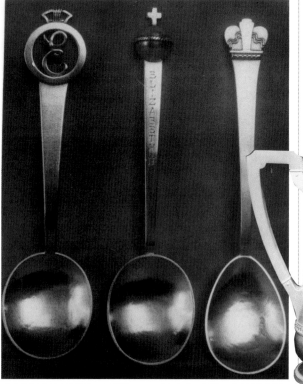

Left: Some of Joyce's work; a spoon set and jug, which is now in the V&A

A distinctive style

On a promotion leaflet of Joyce's, she says *"The traditional use of silver is maintained today, though the design of silverware changes,each original piece being representative o and fulfiling the requirement of that age in which it is produced."*

Some of Joyce's work is very much of the time it was produced, with Art Deco style decoration or embelishments, such as the cigarette box shown on this page.

The many types of work produced by Joyce is amazing, from tiny exquisite jewellery to large functional bowls etc, which she is said by friends to have preferred working on.

Praise in the press

Joyce had many favourable comments and reviews about her work. A few are shown below...

"Joyce R. Himsworth shows a group of exquisite works which again proves- if Sheffield needs such proof- that Miss Himsworth is nothing less than one of our modern masters in the manipulation of gold and silver."
The Sheffield Telegraph, 1933

"Miss Himsworth has already made a name for herself as a designer of special ornaments for use in churches and cathedrals."
Daily Mirror, 1935

"More will be heard of her work. She combines technical excellence of design with an appreciation of what should appeal"
Goldsmiths' Journal, 1937

In the Sheffield newspaper of March 20, 1937 is an article about Joyce Himsworth's work having a special honour:

HONOUR FOR SHEFFIELD CRAFTSWOMAN

Articles selected for Paris exhibition

Miss Joyce R Himsworth... has received intimation from the Department of Overseas Trade that several articles designed and made by her have been selected by the Council of Art and industry of the Board of Trade for display at the Paris International Exhibition, which opens in May. Miss Himsworth is, it is believed, the only Sheffield designer-craftsman whose work has been selected for this exhibition.

A church chalice made by Joyce

Some examples of the variety of work by Joyce

Still remembered

An artistic home

Joyce lived for most of her life, until she died on April 6th, 1989, at a house at Chelsea Road, Nether Edge.

Her father and his brother bought land there in 1908 and had the house and one next to it built specially. Joyce, when she was just 4 or 5, laid the foundation stone bearing her initials, which can still be seen near the front door.

Her father, who seems to be as multi-talented as Joyce, made a stained glass window for the door, with a charming line painting of his young daughter in profile as a centrepiece. The glass bears his initials and the date 1910.

He also painted a frieze around the sitting room of the house, with scenes such as what looks like Saint Michael's Mount in Cornwall and also country lanes and fields.

Joyce R. Himsworth in later years

Scenes from the frieze painted by Joyce's father Joseph

Later, an extension was built at the house for Joyce. A door connected the dwellings. Joyce lived in the main house, however, with her father having the extension, ensuring he was close by to look after him.

Joyce worked in the attic of the main part of the house.

In later life she became friends with David Sier, who lived nearby and had an interest in silversmithing. He and his wife, Angela, helped look after Joyce as she became frail and, when she died, inherited her tools and also kept her order books and papers, which provide a fascinating glimpse into her sketches, commissions and to how busy she was.

Mr. Sier gave some Joyce's work for display in the Millennium Galleries in Sheffield City Centre, to ensure her skill is still admired today (see the panel below).

See some of her work today

Some of Joyce Rosemary Himsworth's work is on display in the Metalwork Gallery in the Millennium Galleries in Sheffield City centre. Exhibited are:

■ a knickerbocker glory spoon (1937) and a pickle spoon (1950),

■ a tiny crucible made and used by Joyce to melt the silver she used

■ a silver and wood saucepan (1950)

■ a silver beaker (1930s) and a silver goblet (1932)

■ a silver hammer and sickle badge

■ a lovely gold and emerald pendant with cutlers emblems

■ a stunning silver comb with a lovely enamel owl on it

■ an opal and gold ring

A pair of gold and enamel cufflinks which were made by Joyce as a birthday present for her father, are also on display in the same case in the gallery.

They show on one cufflink what appears to be a picture of the cup he made (mentioned right) along with his initials On the other cufflink is a knife and spoon design, referencing his cutlery trade. The date in which the cufflinks were made, 1943, is used as a decoration too.

The cuff links that Joyce made for her father

Another gift for her father, in the form of a silver and gilt wristlet, with his name and address (J B Himsworth 31 Chelsea Road Sheffield 11) engraved on it, is also in the cabinet.

On the label for this cabinet is a photo of a painting on vellum of craftsmen, done by Joyce. There is also a silver cup and cover by Joyce's father Joseph on display.

84

Edmund Rd Drill Hall

Just off Queen's Road in Sheffield, tucked away on Edmund Road, is an impressive old military building that has seen many strange sights over the years..

The tower and front of the Drill Hall

The Edmund Road Drill Hall, a red brick, castle-like structure, stands as suggested, on Edmund Road, Sheffield. It was once the headquarters for the 4th West Riding (Yorkshire) Artillery Volunteers and is also known as the Norfolk Drill Hall, named after the Duke of Norfolk, the honorary colonel of these volunteers.

A castle of red brick

The architect of this fine old building was Matthew Ellison Hadfield, whose company also designed the old gas offices and the Victoria Hall on Norfolk Street, Sheffield.

The foundation stone was laid by the Duchess of Norfolk in September 1878, but due to severe winters and hold-ups the opening ceremony wasn't held until June 1880, with a grand dinner and ball.

It was an expensive project and a lot of money was raised by selling shares to the officers.

A grand entrance

The main gate tower is the most impressive part of the building, with it's castellated roof line. Against a blue sky it looks as if it should be in the middle of Italy or Malta. On it is a carved plaque of a shield bearing the arms of the Lord of Hallamshire (the Duke of Norfolk), shown right.

The main entrance, complete with portcullis

The rest of the building is less ornate and a little more functional. On entering the gate tower, the left hand side was once the company office and canteen and on the right was the orderly room, the NCO kitchen and the quartermaster's store. The frontage on Clough Road is the administration part.

On the first floor was the officers' mess, library and kitchen. with bedrooms and toilets.

The roof of the huge hall space inside has impressive metal arches, made by the same company which made the ones for St Pancras railway station in London. When building work was done on the building a few years ago it was found that the base of these arches go at least 15ft into the ground for support.

New additions

In 1889 the drill hall was extended to provide a riding school and stables for the gun carriage horses. Wooden ramps, up which the horses were led to the huge exercise space and riding school on the first floor, are still in place today, as are the stable floors. On the wall of this space is painted the emblem of the artillery, granted in 1832 by King William IV, with the latin motto *"Quo Fas et Gloria Ducunt"*. This translates as *"Where right (or duty) and glory Lead"*.

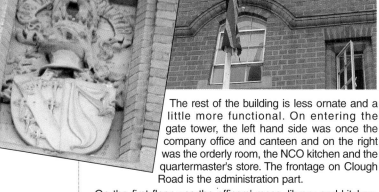

The site of many a show

In the 1920s, when cars had become more common than horses, the horse exercising space was turned into a gymnasium and garages were built at the site. Other regiments used the site at various times.

The last to be there were the 38th Signal Regiment, who then moved to a new base at Manor Top.

For the next ten years the building remained Crown Property, eventually being purchased in 1979, in a derelict state,1979 by a firm called Clarke and Partners, Mobility Specialists.

At the time of writing they still use the ample space enclosed by the red brick walls for their workon cars and making wheelchairs.

The drill hall is now a listed building.

A varied run of events

When the Edmund Road Drill Hall was built it was one of the largest buildings in Sheffield. The potential of the place for exhibitions and shows was used to the full, to help pay for the high running costs.

It could hold up to 12,000, with seating for over 2,000.

Some famous and unusual people and events take their place in the history of this building.

■ The first of Sheffield's dog shows was held here in 1882 and the first motor show in Sheffield in 1900.

■ Samuel Plimsoll, the campaigner for safety at sea who invented the Plimsoll Line (see Peeks at the Past Volume 1) addressed crowds here in 1885.

■ In 1895 there was a waxworks show, and in 1905 a trades exhibition of arts and crafts.

■ During the 1930s the hall was used as a payout station for unemployment benefits and later boxing was also held there.

■ When the country was in conflict during World War Two, the hall became a Home Guard base.

■ In the 1950s it was used for Ideal Home exhibitions.

The exterior of the Drill hall

■ The Drill Hall was also a well known Boxing venue. One of the best atended fights was in 1896, when once famous fighter George Corfield (a former champion of England) met Billy Plummer over 20 rounds. Another was when a boxer named Frank Howson defeated a boxer named Wilson from Leicester and the Drill Hall was absolutely packed.

Above is a Sheffield Newspapers advertisement for a fund raising boxing match at the Drill Hall in World War Two

Blondin walked the rope

Charles Blondin, the famous tightrope walker, performed at the Edmund Road Drill Hall in 1885.

He is still listed in the Encyclopedia Britannica.

Known as 'the daredevil wirewalker, Charles Blondin was a French tightrope walker and acrobat. He was born in St Omar on the 28th February 1824, his real name being Jean Francois Gravelet. At just five years old he was sent to a school for gymnasts at Lyons. Six months later he made his first public appearance as 'the little wonder'.

He toured in a circus troupe, after choosing a new stage name. He choose the name Charles Blondin because of his blonde hair. When the troupe visited America in 1858, he became obsessed with the idea of crossing Niagara Falls on his tightrope. He achieved this first in 1859.

His rope was 1100ft (335m) long and 160ft (48m) above the water. After this crossing he did several more, all with bizarre twists to make them different, including blindfolded, in a sack, pushing a wheelbarrow and carrying a man on his back. He even sat down and cooked and ate an omelette.

In 1861 he first appeared in London at the Crystal Palace, where he did summersaults on stilts - on a rope 170ft up!

In 1862 he was at the Crystal Palace again and toured England.

He retired for a while after this, but emerged again in 1880, giving a final performance in 1896, in Dublin.

He lived for a while at a house in South Ealing in London, which he named Niagara Villa. He died in South Ealing, on 19th February, 1897 and is buried in Kensal Green cemetery.

Blondin also performed at another place during his Sheffield visit. A letter in the local newspaper at a later date, by a TW Willis, says

" I remember seeing ...Blondin walk the tightrope in the Botanical Gardens. What year it was I cannot remember, but it was sometime in the sixties."

Perhaps the most fascinating event held at the Edmund Road Drill Hall was a recreation of an Ashanti Village. The idea of this show now would be totally frowned upon and unacceptable, but to the attitudes of 1902, seeing these people, stuck in a foreign land in the middle of winter and being treated as a circus show as they went about their customs and everyday life to entertain the British, was a great spectacle not to be missed. An advert from the Sheffield Daily Independent newspaper of Friday 12th December, 1902, for the event is shown on the right. An earlier and very patronising article reviewing the event, from the same newspaper, is written

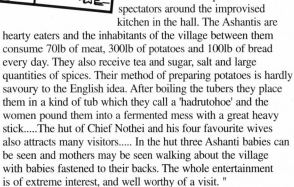

ARTILLERY DRILL HALL SHEFFIELD
FOR A SHORT SEASON ONLY
DAILY, FROM 11A.M to 10P.M.
THE ASHANTEE VILLAGE
NATIVES
100   MEN, WOMEN AND CHILDREN   100
Daily at 4pm and 9pm
MONTE CHRISTO: A DIVE FOR LIFE
THE SENSATION OF THE WORLD
ADMISSION SIXPENCE   Children half-price

The Ashanti Village event was researched by the Friends of the General Cemetery after they had discovered a strange entry in the cemetery burial records. It read:
20.12.1902 Kai Akosia Meusa, age 4 days, daughter of O Meusa, Fisherman, Address Drill Hall, Edmund Rd, Ashantee Village. This was looked into and there was indeed a newspaper entry for December 15th, about the birth:

"Yatso, the first wife of Meusah La, one of the principal warrior dancers in the Ashantee Village, gave birth to a child on Sunday morning. The child has been baptised in native fashion and has been given the name of Kai Akosia, the word Kai meaning that she is the third daughter of the family while Akosia signifies Sunday birth." Sadly the baby did not survive and died four days later, and was buried in the cemetery.

The sketch of the village below is from the Sheffield Weekly Independent of 13 December 1902. Also in this article were these words describing an amazing feat:

"To this exhibition, which concludes this week at the Artillery Drill Hall, Edmund Road, has been added another feature. This is an extraordinary diving feat which is performed each night by Monte Christo. This gentleman is tied, obviously securely, in a sack by one of the audience and in this encumbrance he dives from an altitude of about 70 feet into a tank about 8 feet in diameter, containing only 4 feet of water. In a few seconds he emerges from the water free from the sack.

To make this singular and somewhat dangerous dive he is drawn up to the roof by a contrivance of swings from which he drops into the water feet first."

ASHANTEE NATIVES IN SHEFFIELD

UNIQUE SHOW AT THE ARTILLERY DRILL HALL

"As remarkable an entertainment as has ever been seen in Sheffield during recent years was opened at the Artillery Drill Hall yesterday afternoon. The hall, by the aid of scenery and material imported from the West Coast of Africa, has been turned for the time being into what is stated to be an exact representation of an Ashanti village, in which about a hundred natives of the Gold Coast Territory are living. The natives, a fine looking set of people, are to be seen, during the time the entertainment is open to the public, engaged in their different trades, in cooking, or performing some of the quaint ceremonies peculiar to their country.... The opening ceremony yesterday afternoon was performed by King Nothei,

the chief of the village, assisted by a number of the adult natives. He made a speech, but as it was in his own language, we can only say that in it he greeted those present, said that he and his people came from a far - off country, but that they were all British subjects. Whilst he made the speech, there was held over him a great State canopy with the figure of an elephant on the top. He also went through a ceremony with a glass of rum, part of which he poured on to the ground and part of which he drank. Subsequently he sat in a wickerwork chair, whilst men and girls went through fantastic dances to the accompaniment of weird music from a number of curious drums, iron castanets and mallets. The sound is by no means soothing or seductive, but the performers play with energy and perfect rhythm. The principal dance of the performance - the fetish dance - had to be omitted yesterday as the priest and

priestess were unable to appear due to illness. After the dancing the King was escorted back to his hut in a 'palankin' borne by several young men.

A walk around the village cannot fail to be of interest. In front of a number of the huts is arranged an African bazaar. The first attraction is the workshop of the goldsmith, where clever natives may be seen engraving gold and silver rings and bracelets and ornaments. The rings are generally inscribed with the signs of the zodiac, a characteristic dating from the years when the Portuguese were associated with the Gold Coast. In the Ashanti people the trade of goldsmith ranks higher than all others. The productions of the brassworker, which will next catch the eye, are also worth notice. A carpenter, who was trained at the Basle Mission, does some clever work in wood and ivory carving. A weaver and a calabash carver both attract keen interest. Two of the most remarkable features of the village are the kitchens and the school. Whilst the women were preparing dinner yesterday afternoon there was quite a cluster of spectators around the improvised kitchen in the hall. The Ashantis are hearty eaters and the inhabitants of the village between them consume 70lb of meat, 300lb of potatoes and 100lb of bread every day. They also receive tea and sugar, salt and large quantities of spices. Their method of preparing potatoes is hardly savoury to the English idea. After boiling the tubers they place them in a kind of tub which they call a 'hadrutohoe' and the women pound them into a fermented mess with a great heavy stick.....The hut of Chief Nothei and his four favourite wives also attracts many visitors..... In the hut three Ashanti babies can be seen and mothers may be seen walking about the village with babies fastened to their backs. The whole entertainment is of extreme interest, and well worthy of a visit. "

The Sheffield Weekly Independent Tuesday, Dec 2, 1902

Wirksworth Slab

A detail of the figures carved on the slab

Wirksworth, 4 miles south of Matlock, is an ancient Saxon town, once the lead mining centre of the Peak. It has an ancient church, housing this richly carved stone...

The church of St Mary the Virgin in Wirksworth was founded in 653AD, according to local tradition.
The main fabric of the church is medieval, but there are some Saxon-age stones set within its walls.

Ancient beginnings

At the time of the accepted founding of the church, in 653AD, Bakewell was the major religious centre and also Repton, which still has a wonderful old Saxon crypt.

An old cross

Outside the Church of St. Mary the Virgin, is the shaft of a mediaeval cross, It is standing on what seems to be the base of a much older cross.

The slab

The 'Wirksworth Slab' or stone is a Saxon grave-lid, made of Millstone Grit, that was discovered in the chancel of the church during rebuilding work in 1820. According to church records it was found two feet below the surface, with the carving face downwards. It was over a stone built vault that contained a large human skeleton of a man.

An 'angel' figure on the slab

Unproven tradition around the slab says that it was the coffin lid of Betti, the grandson of Penda, The King of Mercia in 653AD.
He is said to have come to Wirksworth to establish a church.

The slab is made from one large piece of stone, and the carving is of a high standard, with lots of drapery around the figures. The faces of each of the figures are very similar, elongated with pierced eyes. The hands and feet are carved in great detail, as are the wings of the angels, with similar lines to the drapery.

The figures have quite 'pudding basin style', monkish haircuts..

The cross / crucifix has a lamb on it, often used as a symbol of the sacrifice of Christ.

It is likely that this stone was for a Christian person, because of this symbolism and the other possible biblical interpretations of other scenes on the stone, so it could have been for Betti.

The stone is now set into the north wall of the nave of the church, protected from the elements. Some parts of it have been lost and damaged over the years, but the carving was probably protected because it was buried.

A detail of the bottom section of the slab

Detail of the Wirksworth Slab

Christ figure?

The large picture is of the figure widely accepted to be Christ in most interpretations of the slab, including the one in the church guidebook (overleaf).

Some archaeologist think the stone could be given an interpretation other than Christian, however. Left is a picture showing the overall shape of the slab.

The story on the slab

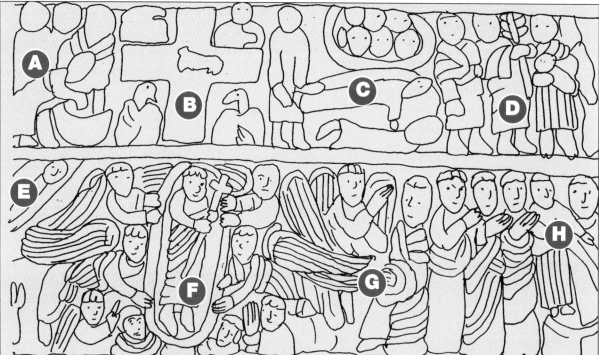

One interpretation is this widely accepted Christian one, found in the church

A. Christ washing the feet of his disciples

B. Crucifixion, showing a lamb and four evangelists

C. The blessed virgin being bourne for burial

D. Christ presented at the temple, the virgin on the right. Simeon holds the child in his arms.

E. Descent into hell. Christ is releasing man. in the form of a baby in swaddling clothes.

All but three souls, Cain Herod and Judas, are released. These three burn in a brazier

F. Christ in an oval panel holds a cross and is being taken to heaven by four angels. The blessed virgin and Saint John are on either side below

G. The blessed virgin, seated, is greeted by the angel of the Annunciation, who carries in his left hand a scroll

H. A figure on the right, probably Saint Peter, stands in a boat (signifying the church), The blessed virgin holds the Christ child on her left arm and he holds a scroll in his right hand, pointing to Peter with his left, to indicate how the word of God is to be transmitted. behind Mary stand a man and a woman, who may be Saint Joseph and Saint Anne

The Church and some more carvings

The church

The church is made of red sandstone, with some limestone.

It stands in a serene green oasis, surrounded by Elizabethan 'Gells Almshouses' and also the Georgian former Grammar School.

An exterior view of the fine old church

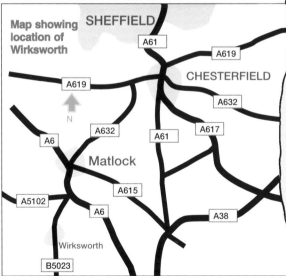

Map showing location of Wirksworth

SHEFFIELD
A61
A619
CHESTERFIELD
A619
A632
N
A632 A61 A617
A6
Matlock
A615
A5102
A6 A38
Wirksworth
B5023

An old tradition

Another old tradition is that of the annual ceremony of clypping (embracing) the church, when a circle of people surround the building, holding hands.

This takes place on the Sunday after the 8th September. The choir and congregation process outside and go around the church singing a hymn. Once the circle is complete, the service continues inside. It is not known when this custom, once more widespread, began, but at Wirksworth it was revived n 1921

T'owd Man

In the wall of the church is set an old stone with a naive style and perfectly charming carving of a lead miner, carrying his little collecting bucket and his tool to dig. He is affectionately known as 'T'owd man' (the old man).

These carvings can also be seen inside the church

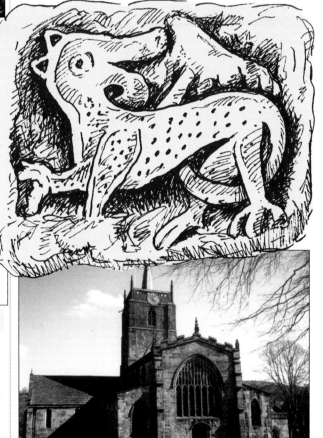

Other attractions in Wirksworth

The town itself

Wirksworth is an intruiging place, with many fine Georgian buildings still surviving. It was one of the 'barmotes' or administration boroughs of the medieval leadmining society.

DH Lawrence, who lived nearby for a year, is said to have called it the 'navel of England'.

There are many fine old buildings, many of which were restored under the "Wirksworth Project' of conservation in the 1980s, which won many awards.

The town also has the tradition of well dressing and a carnival at the Spring Bank Holiday and an art, music and drama festival in September.

Some of the lovely old buildings in Wirksworth

Literary Connections

Wirksworth is also the 'Snowfield' of the Adam Bede novel and was the home of author George Eliot's aunt, Elizabeth Evans, said to be the model for the character of Dinah Bede.

The Barmote Court

Lead mining was carried out in Derbyshire for almost 2000 years, with the peak probably being around 1850.

The ore, called Galena, was even quarried from under the town itself.

The mining is now gone, but many links remain, one of which is the old Barmote Court. In 1288 the 'Barmote Court of the Soke and Wapentake of Wirksworth' was formed, to settle any local lead mining disputes amongst other matters. The court location is at the Moot Hall on Chapel Lane. The Moot Hall was rebuilt in 1812 and the court still meets every year.

A measuring dish for ore, made around 1512, once hung on the wall. Plaques depicting lead mining equipment.

The old Moot hall, home of the Barmote Court

An arresting place

Not far away from The Moot Hall is The Old Lock Up. This was built as a Magistrate's House in 1842. It served as a police station with cells for 100 years, until the 1950s. Now it is an unusual bed and breakfast, still retaining many of the old features, but a lot more home comforts!

Next to the Old Lock Up is a tiny mortuary chapel of rest, where the less spooked guest can also spend a night or two bed and breakfasting.

The neighbours are quiet of course!.

An old cell door inside the Old Lock Up (left) and the old Chapel of Rest nearby (below)

The Heritage Centre

Wirksworth has a very good information source at the Heritage Centre, a former silk and velvet mill in Crown Yard, just off the Market Place.

Wirksworth Diary

Market Day: Tuesday

Early Closing: Wednesday for most, some open six days

Well Dressing: Spring Bank Holiday

Wirksworth Festival: Early September

Art and Architecture Trail: First week of the Festival

Heritage Centre: Open mid February to Easter and November, 11 - 4 Closed Mon/Tues. 1.30-4 Sundays

Easter to Jun and Oct 11 - 4 Closed Mon. 1.30 - 4 Sundays Jul/Aug/Sept 10 - 5 Closed Mon. 1.30 - 5 Sundays. Telephone for exact details

Located at Crown Yard, Wirksworth, Derbyshire, DE4 4ET. Telephone: 01629 825225

Wynne De Lyle

The young Winifred, with her father's dolls

Local woman Wynne spent most of her life entertaining people with her special gift - as a ventriloquist...

Many a 'Tommy' in the war was cheered by the talents of this Sheffield woman, whose life on the stage seems to have been destined from an early age.

A magical father...

Wynne de Lyle was from a family already well used to performance. Her father, George Fox, was a conjuror and ventriloquist, as well as a Punch and Judy man. He was also a talented photographer and gave lantern slide shows.

He was born in Sheffield, on 29 September 1871, the son of John and Anne Fox of Killamarsh. His father had served as a printing apprentice at the firm of Brailsford and then later had his own business as a printer, stationer and newsagent at 126 and 130 Ecclesall Road. George's father was also a lay preacher at the Primitive Bethel Chapel in Cambridge Street, so George became a member of the congregation there too.

George became fascinated with the world of magic when still a boy and gave his first show at the age of 14.

At the age of 21, he inherited the business on his father's death. In 1901 he married Louisa, later having Wynne and her siblings.

George loved his other work, as an entertainer and was looking for a more catchy stage name when he spotted a tin of Lyle's Golden Syrup. He added the 'De' for class, and the title 'Professor', as many Punch and Judy men were referred to ,and became 'Professor De Lyle.'

Bethel Church on Cambridge Street, now a shop, the sign can still be seen near the chimney

He became very well known and entertained at many schools, hospitals and parties. He went to entertain at Chatsworth House, to entertain the children of the Duke and Duchess of Devonshire. Here he performed a trick of smashing a watch he borrowed from a member of the audience, in a bag with a hammer. The unscathed watch eventually reappeared tied with a silken ribbon around the neck of a rabbit, which was produced from a box.

By 1908 the printing business was not doing so well, so he gave it up. The family then moved to a new house a short distance away, at 184 Ecclesall Road, and George began a new career as a grocer, ending up working at the Co-Op as Under-Manager. He carried on performing well into his 70s and died in 1948. The site of the family house at 184 Ecclesall Road is now a small community park.

...and a magical daughter

Winifred Fox was born in Sheffield on 18 September 1903. She was the eldest daughter of George and had three sisters, Madge, Phylis and Elsie and one brother, George junior.

Winnie was always interested in performing and as a little girl she wrote and produced concerts in the back garden at 184 Ecclesall Road for his sisters and brother to take part in.

One of the acts was Elsie and Phylis doing a song and dance routine called 'Little Mr Baggy Britches.' They charged neighbours and entrance fee of two pennies to see the shows, which was given to a poor boys' charity.

WYNNE DE LYLE Premier Lady Ventriloquist
Speciality in "Robinson Crusoe,"
Jan. 31, Pal., Cam. Feb. 7, Hip., Ipswich
P.A., 184, Ecclesall Rd., Sheff., 11

Winnie was also interested in her father's rather unusual occupation and at the age of ten she borrowed his two ventriloquist dolls to do a show of her own, at an end of term concert for her class at school. She had a natural gift and was an instant hit with all the schoolchildren. So much so that her teacher, Miss Unwin, gave her two pennies and asked her to perform in the other five classes.

That was just the beginning. Along with her father she performed her first public concert with him at St Mary's School in Sheffield just a few days later.

It was Christmastime and after the concert she was presented with a doll from Father Christmas and also the then enormous fee of two shillings and sixpence (12.5p).

It was her thoughtful father who had given the money for them to present to her- so that she would be encouraged.

Touring for the 'Tommies'

The following week they did a concert at Cecil Road School, again a success, earning Winnie a huge box of chocolates.

The path of destiny was set and Winnie then did most of her father's concerts with him. He purposely dropped the ventriloquism part of his act so that Winnie could do it instead- under her proud new stage name of 'Little Vinnie De Lyle, a name Miss Unwin had fondly called her at her first show.

In 1914 the First World War broke out and the lives of many was changed forever. Winnie and her father used their gifts to entertain the troops and try and bring a smile to their faces. The two ventriloquist dummies from the show were rechristened 'Sister Susie' and Tommy Atkins.'On Christmas Day 1916, Winnie entertained soldiers at six different hospitals.

Talent contest presents

Around this time, when Winnie was 11, she entered a talent competition at the Tivoli Theatre in Sheffield. Presents were thrown on the stage for her. But in spite of this and the audience cheering for her, she came second, with a boy comedian of 14 taking the top prize, probably because his act had a chorus of soldiers on leave. Winnie was still delighted - as her runner-up prize was two seats to the theatre for a year. Talent scouts wanted young Winnie to be allowed to take to the boards then, but her parents declined as she was too young.

When Winnie was 14, she went to work at the Co-op, which stood just opposite where their house was, where the Safeway supermarket is now. Her father had once worked there too,

A new career

But the world of the theatre beckoned and after offers of work on the stage, Winnie left the Co-op. Carrying her own doll 'Jimmie' in a suitcase, she headed off into the footlights.

She played many theatres and was also a resident entertainer at holiday camps at Norfolk and Skegness. A successful tour included the Channel Islands.

She starred in many pantomimes and was photographed through the years by her father in a variety of theatrical costumes. She also did tricks with paper tearing and folding.

Jimmie today, now living with Wynne's nephew

Winnie also entertained at Christmas parties for children. There is a charming story about one such party, at which the children were invited to kiss Jimmie goodnight as he was put back into his suitcase. After this they had a conversation with 'Santa' who was 'up the chimney' and promised them all sorts of good things if they were good children and went to bed, which they did with no trouble at all. Ventriloquism can be very useful!

During her life Jimmie went everywhere with Wynne, even on holidays. One can only imagine the expression of the customs officers whom Wynne delighted in teasing, by having him say a polite 'How do sir!" as they opened his suitcase.

Cheering the soldiers

Winnie, later called Wynne as she grew up, also entertained troops in World War Two. Jimmie was given his own miniature RAF uniform and used to parachute down onto the stage.

Wynne herself wore a Women's Auxiliary Airforce uniform.

Wynne and Jimmie in their uniforms

On VJ day, Wynne and her father entertained at a celebration party. Wynne had a trick just for the occasion - he screwed up pictures of Hitler and Mussolini, then unwrapped them to reveal instead a picture of Winston Churchill!

Just after the war, Wynne met a man named Herbert Arthur Weller, also involved in the theatre, and they were married on 9 July, 1946, at the Congregational Chapel in Cemetery Road.

An untimely end

Sadly, after just seven years of happy married life, Wynne was killed in a road accident on Watling Street, near Dunstable, in June 1953. She was on her way to Coventry where her relatives lived, to join them in celebrating the coronation of Queen Elizabeth the Second, probably by yet again intending to use her gifts to bring laughter and amusement to others.

■ *Much of the information in this tale was kindly given by Wynne's nephew, David Monks (Wynne's sister Elsie's son), who in turn was told it by his mum and Auntie Phylis. Also information and help was given by Mr George Robson of Halifax.*

Creswell Crags

In a limestone gorge near Worksop, riddled with caves, once roamed woolly mammoth, hyenas and our ancient ancestors, all seeking food and shelter in an age of ice...

A view of the crags at Creswell, shelter for many

Creswell Crags was a perfect place for early people to find shelter. It was one of the most the most Northerly places on Earth to be inhabited in the last Ice Age.

A vital source of food and shelter

This limestone gorge was made around 260 million years ago - at a time called the Permian. It has sedimentary rocks, once at the bottom of sea in the form of mud.

In the last million years the gorge disappeared several times under ice up to a mile thick. Melt water from this ice created the gorge.

The Creswell area was covered in sea water millions of years ago. Geological activity lifted the rocks and also the sea level dropped. The caves were made by water erosion.

There have been about eight ice ages over the last 7,000,000 years. The last one ended about 10,000 years ago.

About 18,000 years ago the ice sheets had reached to about 20 miles away from Creswell Crags. Bleak living conditions made survival hard and any area unaffected by ice was vital to both animals and man. The food, in the form of plants and berries and the water to drink, attracted many kinds of life from many miles away.

In more recent times there used to be a mill and waterwheel at Creswell Crags. This was knocked down to create a duck shooting lake around the 1860s.

Evidence of animals

Remains found at Creswell Crags include those of animals that lived here before last ice age, about 100,000 years ago, when it was warmer.

These include woolly hippopotamus, leopard and lion. During the last ice age. hyenas used the caves as dens.

A Woolly Mammoth. Used as the Creswell Heritage Trust logo

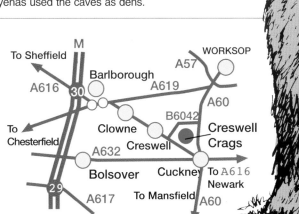

Mammoths died out in Britain about 13,000 years ago, near the end of the last ice age, but survived for longer in Siberia.

Today we know so well what they looked like as complete, frozen and well preserved bodies have been found deep within tombs of ice. Ivory from mammoth tusks were used for spear points. Their huge bones and skins were used to build tent like shelters. They were also of course a food source.

Ancient occupants

Creswell Crags was definitely inhabited during the last ice age, between 70,000 and 1000 years ago. This is known from the plants and animal remains that have been discovered there over the decades.

Neanderthal people were the first humans known to have lived at the crags, during the last ice age. The name Neanderthal is derived from the Neander Valley, which is in Germany. This is where a skull of these people was first found, in 1856, so the people it belonged to were given the name of that area.

These people were skilled hunters, using stone tools, many of which are found at Creswell Crags. The were not primitive as often depicted in early films and books, but made clothes, probably performed ceremonies and buried their dead with flowers. They were capable of beautiful artwork and jewellery

They travelled around looking for food shelter. The Crags were an ideal spot, and they came here at the same time as reindeer and horse herds, to catch them for food.

A Spotted hyena. They lived at the crags

A reindeer. They were hunted by the human as food

Tools

A flint tool

Early people made tools from bones, and used antlers for digging. Bone was also used for other items - a 12.000 year old bone needle was found in Church Hole

Later tools were made from flint. Chippings of flint, caused when tools were made or resharpened, have been found at Creswell. A flint tool is razor sharp, good for cutting and scraping.

Artistic remains from the past

Left is a horse engraving on a bone found in Robin Hood Cave. A notched bone, perhaps once a pendant or hanging decoration was found in Church Hole.

The head of the horse, looking to the right, is highlighted by the red circle

An exciting new discovery

The oldest known art in the country, the first example in Britain of Paleolithic cave art, was found at Creswell Crags, in April 2003. News of it was released in July 2003. The artwork has tentatively been dated, at being around 12,000 years old. Two areas of incised figures were found by archaeologists Dr Paul Bahn and Dr Paul Pettitt from Oxford University and Dr Sergio Ripoll from Madrid.

Creswell Crags was· seen as a good place to look for this previously undiscovered type of art in this country, as

Britain's only figurative engravings on bone, a horse, a human and a reindeer, had been found here in earlier years.

One image of the newly discovered artwork, the clearest, is thought to be that of an ibex (mountain goat) and is more than 50cm wide. It was a surprise to the discoverers as this animal was not thought to have existed in Britain during the ice age or since.

It was hidden by more modern graffiti which had been done over the top of it, dated 1948, 1957, which still looked very new, emphasising how old the ibex drawing below must be.

Photographs courtesy of Creswell Heritage Trust

The ibex, barely distinguishable under much later graffiti. On the right, the shape is outlined to make it clearer

The Crags today

Explorers

Over the decades various people have explored and still explore Creswell, adding to our knowledge of the area.

The Rev. Magens Mello from Brampton was one of the earliest, and explored mainly in Church Hole and Robin Hood Cave. He found bones and some tools in his1876 excavations.

Another explorer was Leslie Armstrong, who was the appointed field archaeologist for the area and conducted his digs in the early 1920's. His most extensive searches were at Pin Hole and Mother Grundy's Parlour.

At Pinhole he found the bones of small mammals and flint chips from making tools. He also found the bones of reindeer, mammoth and woolly rhinoceros, arctic fox and arctic hare.

There is still a huge amount of exploration and discovery to be done at Creswell Crags. Archeological techniques and methods are improving constantly and so giving more detail of the climate and lifestyle during the millennia at Creswell.

More varied information is being collected all the time. For example, well preserved ice age pollen is providing an insight into the plant life all those long years ago and more bones and tools are being uncovered and analysed.

Layout of the area

Today Creswell Crags is classed as a scheduled ancient monument, as well as a geological site of special scientific interest.

Much investment has been put into this precious site over the last few years, to preserve and develop it as a tourist destination and learning resource.

The caves are now all guarded by metal grilles to protect the rare archaeological remains, but visitors can peep through as they walk through the pretty gorge, or take part in one of the special tours, when they can go inside the largest of the caves, Robin Hood Cave.

KEY TO MAP

1. Looking at the Creswell site over 10,000 years ago, the lake would not have been there, but the river would, meandering in the bottom of the gorge. This water supply would have attracted many different species, including mammoth, wild horse, bison, reindeer, lions. wolves. spotted hyenas and people. It was a well protected spot to drink and live

2. Church Hole Cave. The rest of the caves are over the busy road, so take great care in crossing.

3. Entrance to Robin Hood Cave. This is the largest cave, with four main chambers and also over 50 metres of tunnels winding into the cliff.
Tools were found in here, and the drawing on a piece of bone shown on the previous page
In the central chamber Laing found bones of hippopotamus.

This animal was living here 120,000 years ago, before the last ice age. The deepest part of this cave has not been explored yet

4. Entrance to Pin Hole, with a narrow passage into inner chamber

5. Inner chamber of Pin Hole. Armstrong found bones and stone tools here 60,000 to 12,500 years old. The bones had been gnawed by hyenas.

6. Mother Grundy's Parlour. It is not usually possible to visit as it is in undergrowth tucked away.
A local woman told of a dream she had of treasure being found in here.

This has never been proven, though more archeological treasures in the form of hippo bones were found here.

Also Armstrong found lots of flints here and a camp where a wild horse had been butchered to eat.

There is a Museum and Education Centre at the east end of the gorge. Here is an Age of Ice exhibition, as well as stone rubbing, an audio visual show, a gift shop, an activity room with touch screen computers and a hands on area where you can handle replicas of the artifacts.

The site has a picnic area, called Crags Meadow, home to rare grasses and flowers, a perfect place to rest after all that time travel.

The Museum and Education Centre can be found on the B6042 (Crags Road) between the A616 and the A60, one mile east of Creswell village.

There are plans and hopes in the pipeline to improve and rebuilt the centre and also to re-route the B6042 road which cuts through the site.

There are cave tours from the centre, around the gorge to Robin Hood Cave, the largest. These tours take about an hour. Wear boots or shoes with a good grip. Under fives are not admitted to the cave.

There are also many special events, family day activities and themed tours during the year. Ring to find out more information, the times and to reserve a place.

There is also an excellent, award winning 'Virtually the Ice Age' web site about the crags, the address is:

www.creswell-crags.org.uk

Contact details:
Creswell Heritage Trust
Creswell Crags Visitor Centre
Crags Road Welbeck
Worksop, Notts S80 3LH
Telephone: 01909 720378
e mail: info@creswell-crags.org.uk

Museum Opening times:
February - October: Mon-Sat, 10.30am to 4.30pm
November - January: Sunday only, 10.30am to 4.30pm

Old Glass Cone

At Catcliffe, a towering cone shape stands long unused amongst the houses. It is an old glass kiln and can be seen well if you are driving down the Sheffield Parkway...

The distinctive outline of the glass cone

South Yorkshire once had a thriving glass making industry and these cones would have been dotted around the area. Now this one at Catcliffe is the oldest surviving structure of its type in Western Europe and one of only four remaining in the United Kingdom.

Other sites

As mentioned above there were once may other glass works in our area. An article of 22 April 1968, in the Sheffield Telegraph, tells of the others, which included Glass Houghton near Ferrybridge, (closed 1821), Rothwell Haigh near Leeds (1726 - 1773), Whittington near Chesterfield (1704-1807) and Bolsterstone (closed 1778) amongst others.

The Catcliffe Kiln

The Catcliffe site was built about 1740. It was commissioned and owned by a man called William Fenny, who had previously been a manager of the glass works at Bolsterstone.

The cone before it was restored

The cone stands 50ft high and has a diameter of 36ft. The height helped produce a draught of air through the furnace which increased the heat generated by the fire. Fuel was in the form of coal.In the mid nineteenth century, the works produced jugs, vases and flasks decorated with opaque white strips like the style of Nailsea glass. Sheffield City Museum holds some examples of Catcliffe Glass ware.

The works closed sometime between 1884 and 1887. The site was briefly reopened in 1900. This late usage of the site is probably the reason it survived so well.

It is said that prisoners of war were housed in the cone in the First World War and that during the 1926 strikes, it was used as a canteen for feeding children.

An article in The Star Newspaper of 30 May 1963 also says that the cone had been used for the occasional barn dance.

A Narrow Escape

The old cone was threatened with demolition in the 1960's as it was subjected to a lot of vandalism and thought to be a liability and unsafe. Because it was in danger of being lost, it was excavated in 1962 by a six strong unofficial archeological team. They found lots of waste glass.

The glass cone was saved, however, when, in May 1963, it was 'unhesitatingly recommended' that it was given scheduled monument status, which protected it a little.

At the time it stood in a garden of a house belonging to a man called Charles Jackson, a former naval engineer. He was relieved when it was scheduled as it was too much for him to look after. There was still controversy and the debate split the council in 1964 as they couldn't decide if it was a monument or a 'monster'. In November 1969 a local councillor wanted to pull it down as it was thought to be a danger to children. Luckily, the cone was bought by the Council and so survived.A £5000 facelift was carried out in 1973. Work halted for a while though during the project, as there was a difference of opinion over the correct type of sand to use. It has now been restored again and stands in the midst of houses. Access is from Main Street.

The archeological dig at the site

Wardsend Cemetery

Behind the racing dogs and bikes of Owlerton Stadium and the sweet factory home of Bertie Bassett is a little visited cemetery with a dark past...

A view from Wardsend, over Hillsborough & Owlerton

The old Cemetery at Wardsend is at the foot of Old Park Wood, between the railway line and the River Don, on Club Mill Road.

Burial ground beginnings

In June 1857, the Rev. John Livesey M.A., who had been appointed vicar of nearby St. Philip's Church in 1831, acquired 5 acres of ground at Wardsend for a new burial ground because the St Phillip's one was set to close. The land was in a pretty wooded area, on a steep hillside near the then new railway line for Manchester and Lincolnshire. A lodge and chapel (right) were erected there at a cost of £2,600.

On the 21st of June 1857, the churchyard of St. Philip's Church, was closed, except for family vaults in which burials continued until the 27th of March 1918. After that the burials took place at Wardsend Cemetery. It was consecrated on 5th of July 1859, by Archbishop Musgrave of York.

By the 1890s too many people had been buried there and it was getting full, so in 1901, a further 2 acres of land on the other side of the railway were added. So Wardsend Cemetery is unusual in that it has a railway line through the middle of it.

Bodysnatching

Wardsend has a dark and grisly tale associated with it. In June 1862, the sexton there, Isaac Howard, was accused by a labourer at the nearby tannery, Robert Dixon, of bodysnatching. Dixon alleged that Howard was digging up corpses to sell to the medical school. Dixon had gone into the stable block of the house after noticing an unpleasant smell. To his horror he found 22 coffins and 24 coffin name plates in there. He reported this to the police and after investigating they also found a pit full of decomposing bodies.

People got to hear of this and there was a riot, with the chapel stoned and Howard's house near Hillsborough Park torched. Relatives of people buried in the cemetery were given rods so they could prod their loved one's grave and ensure the coffin was there.

Howard was taken away with a police escort. He was tried at York Assizes after being found at Buxton, and convicted of unlawfully disinterring bodies. There was no evidence that he had actually sold any of the bodies to the medical schools or elsewhere. He was imprisoned for six months.

The Rev. Livesey, was also implicated in the scandal because he had not observed the proper administrative procedures and had issued false certificates of burial. He too was tried at York Assizes and was sentenced to three weeks in prison, but only served a week. He returned to his work in the parish until he died in 1870.

There are many decorative gravestones at Wardsend

Some of the people buried at Wardsend

Flood victims

This burial ground is home to some of the 240 victims of The Great Sheffield Flood of the night of 11th/12th of March 1864, when the Dale Dyke reservoir at Bradfield, collapsed. These included the children of Paymaster Sergeant Foulds of Hillsborough Barracks, Isabella, aged 5 and John, aged 3. Also here are a Mr. Joseph Goddard and his wife Sarah, of Malin Bridge.

James Lee

This man was a well known bible reader and a member of the Philadelphian Wesleyan church.

The stone was given by young men and women of his bible class, as a token of their esteem.

James Lee's stone is off to the left of the main path up as you come up the steps on entering the cemetery

Skilled work

As you wander looking at the graves, it is a pleasure to notice the lovely details carved on many by the skilled stone masons.

This acorn design forms a border on some of the headstones.

Tale of an American Indian

One of the stories told about Wardsend is that an American Indian from Buffalo Bill's Wild West Show is buried here.

I 1891, Bill Cody did indeed bring his show tothe area which is now the dog track. It was a great success, but unfortunately one of his performers. Paul Eagle Star. an American Indian, fell and hurt his leg. It was not broken but he developed blood poisoning and had to have the limb removed. The operaton did not save him, however and he died four days later.

There was an inquest, which some of Eagle Star's friends attended, including 'Kicking Bear' and 'Bull Stands Behind'.

The verdict was accidental death and his body was put on a train to Nottingham, where the show was by then performing.

Paul Eagle Star was then taken for burial in Bromton Cemetery in London, not buried at Wardsend, though this was near to where he had his accident. He was eventually reunited with his far off homeland - in 1998 he was taken back to America by relatives.

Publicans

A relatively grand monument belongs to a family by the name of Adamson, who were publicans at the Ball Inn pub which once stood on Green Lane.

This carving is found on a gravestone near the newer part of the cemetery, at the top of the hill. The owner died whilst at his favourite fishig spot

A sad accident

As the work is done to clear some of the undergrowth from the cemetery, new graves are being discovered all the time.

One recently found is that of a young man who died in an accident on Christmas Day in 1877. The stone reads:

"In affectionate remembrance of George Beaumont who was accidentally killed whilst playing at football. December 25th 1877. Aged 23 years."

"In the midst of life we are in death. A sudden change in a moment fell And not time to bid my friends farewell. Think this not strange, Death happens to us all. Tisday was mine, tomorrow you may fall."

The stone was erected by the Members and Friends of The Walkley and Owlerton Broughton Football Clubs.

The Friends of Wardsend cemetery traced this story to the Star and Daily Times newspaper of Thursday, December 27 1877:

THE FATAL ACCIDENT IN A QUARRY AT WALKLEY

To-day an inquest was held at the Freedom House Inn, Walkley, beforeMr Wightman, the borough Coroner, upon te body of George Beaumont, forger, Owlerton, who was killed on Christmas Day, through inadvertently leaping into Mr John Nadin's quarry after a football. The quarry is situated in the field used as a football ground by th St Philip's Club......

....In the course of the game the ball was kicked over the wall into the quarry and the deceased, who did not know of the difference in the level between the quarry and the field at this part, ran and jumped on to the top of the wall. One or two of the stones gave way and he fell into the quarry, a distance of between sixty and eighty feet."

A few views of the cemetery

More decorative details

This gravestone is one of the most ornately carved ones in the cemetery

An open bible carved on one of the stones and (right) a dove bearing an olive branch

Military connections

Because it stands so close to Hillsborough Barracks, the Wardsend Cemetery has many military personnel buried in its grounds.

The obelisk monument, shown below right, commemorates the soldiers of 6th, 19th, 24th, 33rd, 51st, 55th Regiments of Foot. It stands near the site of the old chapel.

It is in memory of those who died whilst at Hillsborough Barracks during the period 1866 - 1869.

A separate grave belongs to Lieutenant George Lambert V.C., (shown below). He was an Irishman, born in Markethill, County Armagh, in December 1819.

The gravestone of Lieutenant George Lambert, VC

Lambert was a sergeant in the 84th Regiment (York & Lancaster Regiment) and was promoted twice without purchase and was awarded his Victoria Cross for conspicuous bravery during the Indian Mutiny at Oonao in 1857.

His death was due to the breaking of a blood vessel whilst he was on the parade ground of Hillsborough Barracks on February 10th 1860, when he was 39 years old.

In the Sheffield and Rotherham Independent newspaper of February 18th, 1860, is an account of his funeral:

"The ceremony was conducted with military honours, the band of the regiment marching at the head of the procession and playing the 'Dead March.' ....
his charger was led after the body,
bearing his master's boots reversed.
The usual volleys were fired over his
grave at the conclusion of the service
and the procession then returned to
the barracks."

There are also memorials to several soldiers who gave their lives during both World Wars, including one from a naval officer of the Drake Battalion.

The ste of the old chapel and the site of the obelisk in memory of Barrack personnel

The cemetery today

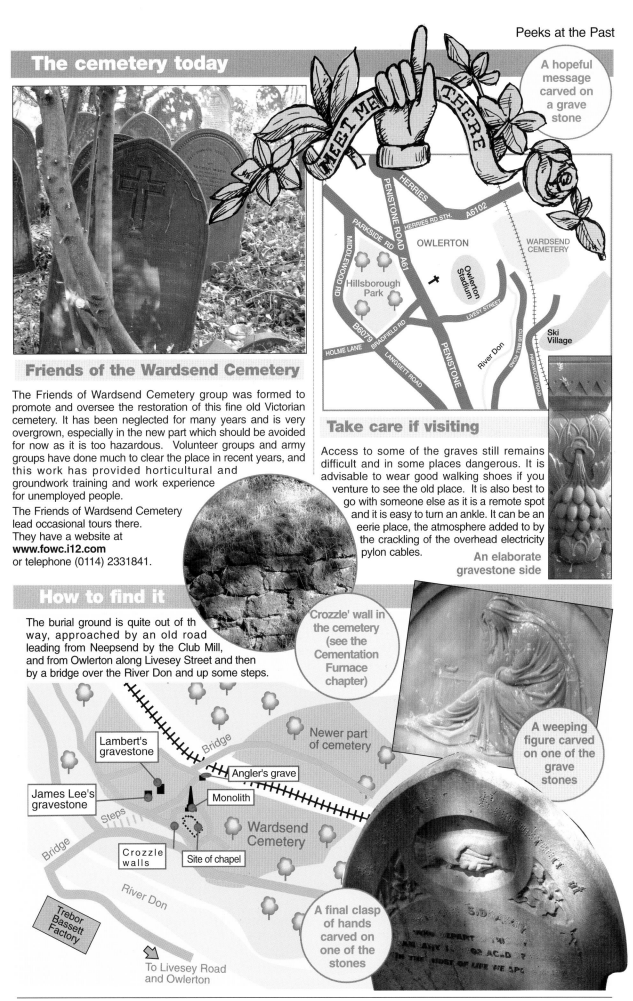

A hopeful message carved on a grave stone

Friends of the Wardsend Cemetery

The Friends of Wardsend Cemetery group was formed to promote and oversee the restoration of this fine old Victorian cemetery. It has been neglected for many years and is very overgrown, especially in the new part which should be avoided for now as it is too hazardous. Volunteer groups and army groups have done much to clear the place in recent years, and this work has provided horticultural and groundwork training and work experience for unemployed people.

The Friends of Wardsend Cemetery lead occasional tours there.
They have a website at
www.fowc.i12.com
or telephone (0114) 2331841.

Take care if visiting

Access to some of the graves still remains difficult and in some places dangerous. It is advisable to wear good walking shoes if you venture to see the old place. It is also best to go with someone else as it is a remote spot and it is easy to turn an ankle. It can be an eerie place, the atmosphere added to by the crackling of the overhead electricity pylon cables.

An elaborate gravestone side

How to find it

The burial ground is quite out of th way, approached by an old road leading from Neepsend by the Club Mill, and from Owlerton along Livesey Street and then by a bridge over the River Don and up some steps.

Crozzle' wall in the cemetery (see the Cementation Furnace chapter)

A weeping figure carved on one of the grave stones

Lambert's gravestone

James Lee's gravestone

Angler's grave

Monolith

Crozzle walls

Site of chapel

Newer part of cemetery

Wardsend Cemetery

Steps

Bridge

Bridge

River Don

Trebor Bassett Factory

To Livesey Road and Owlerton

A final clasp of hands carved on one of the stones

Mount Pleasant

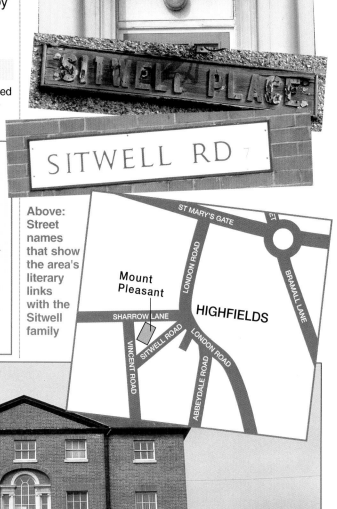

A grand doorway at the old house

Near Highfields in Sheffield, just off London Road, is a fine old building that was once a home for a member of a famous literary family...

Mount Pleasant is a lovely old mansion that is now used as a community centre. Once it was used as a second home by Sitwell Sitwell, of the same family as the famous and eccentric Dame Edith Sitwell.

A varied past

The association of the place with the Sitwell family is reflected in the street names around the area. Through the years the building at Mount Pleasant has had many different uses, some of which are listed below:

1786	Known as Brightfield House. Designed and built by John Platt, a Rotherham Architect
1793	Sitwell Sitwell used it as a second home
1794	Sold it to Samuel Broonhead Ward
1849	It was let to Thomas Tillotson
1872	It became a school
1939	It became bank clerk offices then had a multiple occupancy, used by school board
1963	It was an MOT driving test centre
1968	Used by the Department of Social Security
1971	Almost pulled down but saved
1974	A Community Centre is planned
1978	The Community Centre is opened

Above: Street names that show the area's literary links with the Sitwell family

The old house known as Mount Pleasant, now a community centre

The Sitwell family

The Sitwell family became famous through the works of Edith, Osbert and Sacheverell, the three children of Sir George and Lady Ida Sitwell. The youngest was known as 'Sachie'. He was the only one of his generation to marry, and Renishaw Hall in Derbyshire now belongs to his elder son, Sir Reresby Sitwell.

The Original Manor was built in 1625 andl has been the home of the Sitwell family for over 350 years. The beautiful Italianate garden, park and lake were the creation of the eccentric Sir George Sitwell, grandfather of the present owner.

It is worth a trip there as the gardens are lovely and there is also a stableyard cafe and restaurant, as well as an art gallery showing the works of John Piper, a museum dedicated to the theatre and also a museum dedicated to the Sitwell family.

In summer swallows sweep over the gardens and courtyard. There is a good website about the hall at www.sitwell.co.uk

Dame Edith Sitwell (1887-1964)

The is the most famous of the family and was much painted and photographed, her unusual appearance being a striking subject. Edith's style of dressing and eccentricity gained her initial fame and notoriety in the social circles of the time. From 1916 to 1921 she edited 'Wheels', an annual anthology of modern verse. Some of her own poems were recited to the music of William Walton. One, called 'Façade', where she read through a megaphone-like device., caused much debate amongst critics. She was friends with Virginia Woolf and others from the London Bloomsbury group of artists and writers.

www.edithsitwell.com is a website devoted to her life and works. She died in London in 1964. During the war, she retreated from the public gaze and lived with her brother Sir Osbert in the family estate of Renishaw Hall. She wrote poems about the impact of the war, the most acclaimed being Still Falls the Rain (1942), which describes an air raid in London, during the blitz. In later years, her work became more popular again, especially in America. She was made a Dame of the British Empire in 1954.

Sir Osbert Sitwell (1892-1969)

He wrote poetry, short stories, novels. In later years, recognised as a Grand Old Man of English Letters, he continued to write and also looked after the management of the Renishaw Estate and served as a Justice of the Peace.

Sir Sacheverell Sitwell (1897-1988)

His first volume of poetry The People's Palace was published in 1918, but he is best known for his writing on the arts.

Around Mount Pleasant

The two heads on the below and right are from an old bank, now Rossi's Italian Restaurant

The two heads left are from a buildng that fronts onto London Road

Mount Pleasant, with the Hallamshire Hospital in the background

Wingfield Manor

The grand entrance of Wingfield Manor still survives

Wingfield Manor is a ruined, mid 15th century mansion, standing high on a hill overlooking the village of South Wingfield...

This once grand manor was built by Ralph, Lord Cromwell, the treasurer of England, in about 1440, on the site of a 12th century castle.

A splendid old building

The manor was once a splendid residence and had a large main hall. This is now roofless and ruinous but a bay window and the porch at the manor still survive.

The High Tower is still there too and gives a lovely view over the ruins. Part of the old hall chapel still remains also.

The gatehouses into the hall have a large and a small archway, large for vehicles, small for people on foot.

Under the main hall is an impressive undercroft or cellar. It is vaulted and has heavy stone ribs springing from columns down the middle. Where the ribs meet there is an ornate boss as a centrepiece. There are entrances into here from both inside the building and outside, so it is quite likely to have been used as a storeroom.

There are bags of purses of stone carved over the gateway leading to the hall, further emphasising that the builder was Ralph, Lord Cromwell, the Treasurer of England

There are three huge fireplaces, two with ovens, in what was the kitchen area, as well as serving hatches in the wall.

The captive Queen

Mary Queen of Scots was imprisoned at Wingfield Manor, among many other places, her captor being the Earl of Shrewsbury, who held the manor at that time.

It is said that it was here that the plot to free Mary and overthrow Elizabeth I was hatched. Mary is also said to have often spent time looking out from the tower.

Wingfield continued to be the occasional residence of the Shrewsburys until 1616.

A lovely old window, and a view of the ruins

From besieged to film set

Civil war connections

The hall owes the fact that it is now in ruins to the Civil War. When the Civil War started in 1642, the manor was fortified and was a strongly garrisoned base for Royalists coming to the area. In June 1644 Parliament's forces, decided to take the manor and camped outside the walls.

On 14 August the walls were breached by their guns and the garrison inside surrendered, a siege of 10 weeks ended. After the surrender of King Charles in 1646, Parliament ordered the manor to be dismantled so it could not be used for defence again. This began the process of its ruination. There are cannonball holes in the walls at Wingfield Manor, to remind us of those troubled times.

Wingfield Manor has long been seen as an attractive tourist location. Pawson and Brailsford's Guide to Sheffield of 1879 tells us:

"The ruins may be seen from the railway between South Wingfield and Ambergate. It is often visited from Matlock Bath. Rhodes the author of "Peak Scenery," recommends a visit to Wingfield in preference to any other excursion from Matlock, prescribing the route from Cromford along the Derby road to Whatstandwell Bridge, thence up the steep hill to Crich, from which Wingfield is two miles distant, returning by Crich Cliff, Holloways and Lea Bridge. He says 'the distance there and **back is twelve miles and twelve miles of greater and rarer beauty are not often travelled over"**

A popular film set

Wingfield Manor is a very romantic ruin and makes a wonderful film location. Among the productions that have taken advantage of the atmosphere of the place are 'Peak Practice' and Zeffirelli's 'Jane Eyre'. Zeffirelli used the ruins as the burned out 'Thornfield' home of Mr Rochester. Haddon Hall was used as his home before the fire.

The crypt of the manor featured in a 1980s BBC production of The Chronicles of Narnia by CS Lewis, when it was turned into the witches palace.

Opening times

Wingfield Manor is open throughout the year except 24th to 26th December and 1st January. Closed between 1 and 2 pm in the winter. Telephone (01773) 832060 for more details and times.

Parking is on the road and there is a 5 minute walk up to the Manor. Wingfield Manor is looked after by English Heritage and there is an admission charge. (The manor is set within a private working farm. There can be no visiting outside of official opening hours).

Peeks at the Past

Keppel's Column

Keppel's column, standing in Scholes Coppice

A tall tower stands proudly over a housing estate, in recognition of a man's honour being returned after a mistaken slur...

In a field behind bungalows in Admiral's Crest, just off the A629, stands the feature known as Keppel's Column, in Scholes Coppice.

Who was Keppel?

Admiral Keppel was a friend of Charles, the Marquis of Rockingham and he supported of the Whig party which Charles led.

In 1778, Keppel was charged with cowardice in a naval defeat at the hands of the French in the previous year, 1777.

Keppel and another man, Sir Hugh Palliser, were tried at a Court Marshall and gained honourable acquittals.

Palliser resigned after the trial, but Admiral Keppel went on to become First Lord of the Admiralty.

The Marquis of Rockingham had always believed in his friend and to celebrate the acquittal he started work on building a column, to honour Keppel. He had already wanted to build a tower and adapted the design he had in mind already.

The column built stands at 35 metres (115 ft) high, but it was originally planned to be even taller and capped with a statue of Admiral Keppel. The base and pedestal 6.9 m (23 ft) square. There is a spiral staircase inside the tower, which people used to climb for a small fee, to admire the view.

A third of the way up the staircase, at the widest point of the column, is a room with seats to have a rest.

The column was restored in the 1900s. It was open to the public until the 1960s before it became too dangerous to climb. Now it is again in need of restoration

Though it is not possible to get up or near to the tower, a good view can be gained from the path running from Admiral's Crest.

"Another curve in the road and through a little copse on the right, with high quarries of many-tinted stone on the left, we come to the old and well known inn called 'Bellhag'. From the parlour of this inn and the rocks beyond and in front of it, magnificent views of Rivelin are obtained. In the afternoon, when the westering sun shines on Keppel's Pillar, it may be seen from the Bellhag towering like a line of light over Wentworth's halls."

A description of a walk from Pawson and Brailsford's guide to Sheffield of 1879

PHOTO: DENNIS LOUND, Sheffield Newspapers

A photograph of Keppel's Column from the air

Scholes Coppice

The place where the column stands is also important historically. The name is taken from a nearby settlement, the village of Scholes just to the north. The Coppice is probably an 'ancient woodland', meaning that it has probably been there for 400 years at least. The mixture of plants in a wood is an indicator used to decide this and the coppice has many of the plants associated with a long established woodland, usually those that spread relatively slowly. Bluebells, Wood Anemone, Wood Sorrell and Ramsons are some of these plants. The woodland has been used for timber and pheasant shooting through the years.

Wood Anemone (right) and Ramsons (far right)

108

Ecclesall Church

The impressive edifice of the church from Ecclesall Road South

The fine church of All Saints at Ecclesall Road South in Sheffield is hard to miss, as it towers over the traffic and passes by, like some vast cliff...

The church of All Saints on Ecclesall Road South is one of the most impressive buildings in the area. Looking up at it from Silver Hill (so named because a hoard of silver coins were found there), it seems to grow from the ground like a mini mountain, reminiscent of Lindisfarne Castle.

A familiar edifice

The first building of worship on the site was a small chapel in the 13th century. This chapel was founded by a man called Ralph de Ecclesall, a descendant of Robert Fitz Ranulph, the founder of Beauchief Abbey. Ralph made an endowment in his will to provide funds for the chapel to be built. The chapel was served by the canons of Beauchief Abbey, until the dissolution of the abbey in 1536.

After this time, the chapel was closed and left derelict for decades, until 1622, when the Vicar of Sheffield, Mr Toller, agreed to pay his son-in-law £5 per annum to minister at Ecclesall.

The small chapel, back in use and becoming more popular for a growing population, soon became too small. Money was raised to build a new, bigger church. The foundation stone of this bigger church, which still forms the nave of the building there today, was laid in June 1787. The church was opened in December 1788 and consecrated in 1789. It was described as 'factory like' because of the large, plain design.

Interior, (left) and one of the stained glass windows (in circle)

A view up at the church from Silver Hill

Autumn view of the lovely entrance from Ringinglow Rd

More changes

In 1843, there were a lot of alterations to the church. The upper and lower windows were joined by cutting out the stone between them and adding more glass, lancet arches and mouldings were added for a little embellishment and the tower was raised, with a pseudo Norman doorway added at its base.

More changes arrived in 1908, after the vicar then, Rev. Thomas Houghton, made more enlargements to the building. Much of the imposing exterior we see today is due to these alterations. The transept and chancel were added to make it a cruciform building and galleries removed. The new extensions were in a more elaborate style than the ' factorylike' appearance of the rest of the church, with arches and a vaulted roof. The nave, the oldest part, was left unaltered. The architect for this work was a Mr Temple Moore, and the cost, including the rebuilding of the organ, was £10,000.

It was intended that the unaltered parts would be rebuilt too, to tie in with the new, but the start of World War 1 put an end to such projects. The resulting Depression and then World War Two were more hard factors for the country and by the end of the war building projects were much more controlled and costly, with many other rebuilding projects fighting for priority.

In 1964 a new roof and a new heating system were installed and redecorating was done.

The building plans of Rev Houghton never happened, so the interior of the church still has its contrasting styles. Much re-ordering took place in 1998. The church has chairs not pews, making it a flexible space used for all kinds of performance as well as for worship. It is a welcoming and very alive place, with a modern and airy foyer space, and gallery seating. Modern additions at home with the old.

Views of the tower and doorway

The wall monument in the church and the chest tomb in the graveyard for John Rodgers of Abbeydale House (see first chapter of this book)

Famous people

Many of Sheffield's great and good have been buried at All Saint's. Inside is a tablet wall memorial to William Shore, who died in 1822 , and his wife Mary. Their son assumed the name of Nightingale and was the father of Florence Nightingale.

Also in the church is a monument to John Rodgers of Abbeydale House. His tomb is in the churchyard, as are those of John Brown of Endcliffe Hall and William Butcher of the Butcher Works.

The graves of John Brown (top) and William Butcher

Other stones and carvings

ALICE WILSON.

On this page are some of the lovely carvings and gravestones to be found in the churchyard

Services at All Saints

Sundays: Holy Communion 10.30am 6.30pm

Wednesdays: Holy Communion 10.30am

For other service times and information look at the website:**www.ecclesall.parishchurch.org.uk**

Ecclesall Local History Society sometimes take guided walks around the graveyard. Telephone 236 0245 for details.

Grouse and Trout

A carved stone lies by the roadside at one of the beauty spots on Sheffield's outskirts

If you have ever been out walking or driving near the Redmires Reservoirs, you may have spotted an old inscribed stone by the side of the road. The stone has three trout and a grouse carved on it and is the last remnant of a once popular public house.

A place of refreshment

When the dams for the reservoirs at redmires were built to supply water to the rapidly expanding population of Sheffield, there were of course many workers on the site for several years. They were doing a hard and thirsty job and in the 1840s two beer houses opened at farmhouses nearby to give them a much needed source of refreshment. It is not hard to guess that these beer houses did very well. They were run by farmers who had taken out licences and brewed the beer for sale to supplement their income. The two beer houses were called The Grouse and Trout (after the main shooting and fishing occupations in the area) and Ocean View (probably because the huge dams did indeed look like an ocean).

At first the pubs were used solely by the dam workers, who packed them out at night before returning to their tents, (if they could still walk). Later on though ramblers started venturing out to look at the new dams and they used the pubs too, taking in a jar as they wandered around Stanage Edge and the moors.

By 1885 other farmers had taken out licences and started beer houses, at The Three Merry Lads and Sportsman, which are still there as public Houses today.

Old stone sign from the Grouse and Trout

ISB 1828

ICH DEIN DINNER

SITE OF GROUSE AND TROUT
SITE OF OCEAN VIEW
To Sheffield
Redmires Reservoirs
Long Causeway
To Stanage Pole

The first two beer houses did not survive the years. The Ocean View got less popular because of the other competition and closed in 1885. The Grouse and Trout did too well. By 1913 trips out to the moors in motor cars had become more commonplace and the hoardes of people arriving became too much for the landlord, who decided to have his licence revoked. After this the place served tea and cakes for a while but was eventually demolished.

The stone still there today is the old pub sign. Under the carving of the trout and grouse is the once totally appropriate latin inscription; "Ich Dein Dinner" (I serve dinner).

The Long Causeway was a Roman Road and parts of it are still intact, between the Redmires Reservoirs and Stanage Pole, another old wooden way marker for crossing the moors.

Nick Lister of Sheffield and District CAMRA (Campaign for Real Ale) researched this pub. For more details about CAMRA telephone (0114) 2497708. Their website is www.sheffieldcamra.co.uk. Enquiries by e-mail to membership@sheffieldcamra.co.uk

Stanage Pole and part of the long causeway

Barncliffe Stoop

On Redmires Rd, opposite Hallam Grange Road and next to a bustop, is an old stone, which is a Grade II listed monument called Barncliffe Stoop. It is a 6ft tall skyline marker that is believed to have been erected before 1500. It was one of a series of stones that marked the way to Sheffield across open moorland.

These stones were put at the top of hills or where they could be seen easily, to guide travellers when there were no nice easy road signs or maps to follow. Stoop stones are markers and don't usually have any mileage on them, but this one has a milestone, added later.

About 150 years ago the milestone was stolen but it was discovered in the City Museum basement in 2002. Local enthusiasts formed the Barncliffe Stoop Restoration Group and raised £1200 to make an exact

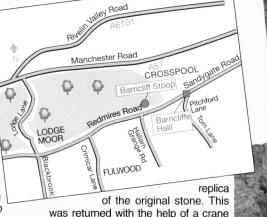

Rivelin Valley Road
A6101
Manchester Road
A57
CROSSPOOL
Barncliff Stoop
Sandygate Road
Pitchford Lane
Lodge Lane
Barncliffe Halll
Tom Lane
LODGE MOOR
Redmires Road
Hallam Grange Rd
Blackbrook
Crimicar Lane
FULWOOD

replica of the original stone. This was returned with the help of a crane and put in place with the stoop in 2002

Barncliffe Stoop

Thanks to...

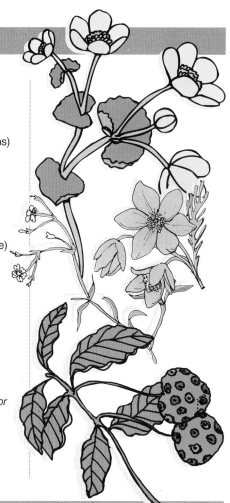

Norman Salt (Barmouth Antiques)
Bob Bone (Endcliffe Hall)
Ian Wall at Creswell Heritage Trust
Maurice Robson
David Monks
David Siers
Natalie Murray
(Sheffield Industrial Museums Trust)
James Symonds, ARCUS
John Bailey
Malcolm Nunn
Peter Quincey
Julia Hatfield
Ian Hollin (Handsworth Church)
John Pitts
Handsworth Sword Dancers)
Fire and Police Museum staff
Roche Abbey staff
Kim Streets Sheffield City Museum
Local History Library staff
Edward Baker
Cath Parker
Nicola Hale
Dennis Lound
The Star Newspaper
Tanya Schmoller

Henk Littlewood - Friends of the
General Cemetery
Jan Alton - Medical Herbalist
Alan Powell
Philipa Godfrey (Botanical Gardens)
Michael Clarke
Cynthia Ramsden
(Fanshawe Gate Hall)
Father Simon Griffiths
(St Matthew's Church)
Mike Trott and Gareth Roberts
(Friends of Abbeydale Picture House)
Graham Lee (at Wingfield Manor)
Don Hughes (Wirksworth
Team Ministry)
Mr CJ Stokes (Stokes Paints)
Paul Fletcher
Norman Trott (Steetley Chapel)
Ecclesall Parish Church
Ecclesall local History Group

and any others I have spoken with or
had help from whom I may have
neglected to mention

Useful websites, addresses & telephone numbers

www.sheffieldtoday.net
(The Star Newspaper's website)
www.simt.co.uk
(Sheffield Industrial Museums trust)
Telephone 0114 2722106
www.tilthammer.com
A site about local people and industry
www.english-heritage.org.uk
Tel: (0870) 333 1182
www.genuki.org.uk
(Sheffield Places, photos etc.)
www.sorby.org.uk
Sorby Natural History Society
www.picturesheffield.com
(A collection of old photographs
from the library archives)
www.shu.ac.uk
(Public Art Archive)
www.victorian-society.org.uk
Tel: (020) 8994 1019
www.sbg.org.uk
The Botanical Gardens, Sheffield
www.fgh.org.uk
A website about Fanshawe Gate Hall
www.fowc.i12.com
Wardsend Cemetery site

■ Fletchers Bakery
Claywheels Lane (0114) 2348171
■ Sheffield Archives
52 Shoreham Street
Sheffield S1 4SP (0114) 2039395
■ Public Art Slide Library,
David Ball 2252721
■ Sheffield Visitor Information Centre:
(0114) 2211900
■ Sheffield Central Lending Library
(0114) 2734729
■ Alton & James Medical Herbalists
253 Sharrowvale Road, S11 8ZE
Telephone (0114) 2682468
■ St Matthew's Church
(0114) 2305641
■ The Friends of Abbeydale
Picture House
office 375 Abbeydale Road
(0114) 2550172
■ Bradfield Parish archives and Family
History Centre
(0114) 2851375
■ The Fire and Police Museum
(0114) 2491999
■ St Mary's Handsworth Parish Centre
(0114) 2692537
■ The Cross Keys Pub, Handsworth
(0114) 2541050

■ Wirksworth Heritage Centre
(0114) 01629 825225
■ Wingfield Manor
(01773) 832060
■ Creswell Heritage Trust
(01909) 720378
■ Clarke & Partners Mobility
(0114) 2755000
■ Stokes Paint
(0114) 2589595
■ Traitional Heritage Mueum
605 Ecclesall Road Sheffield
(0114) 2226296

Stone faces peer from corners;
a winged dragon perches
lightly on a sill.
Forgotten hands that
wrought them
give us pleasure still

Quotes about Sheffield...

Sheffield has of course changed much over the centuries and the city centre is undergoing a big regeneration, with every kind of 'quarter' coming into being. Here are quotes telling what three people thought of the old Sheffield- some of them enough to make a tourism officer weep..

George Orwell
ROAD TO WIGAN PIER DIARIES'

2 March:

"At Wallace Road, Sheffield. Thick snow everywhere on the hills as I came along. Stone boundaries between the fields r unning across the snow like black piping across a white dress."......

"Had a very long and exhausting day being shown every quarter of Sheffield, on foot and by tram. I have now traversed almost the whole city. It seems to me, by daylight, one of the most appaling places I have ever seen. In whichever direction you look you see the same landscape of monstrous chimneys pouring forth smoke which is sometimes black and sometimes of a rosy tint said to be due to sulphur. You can smell the sulphur in the air all the while. All buildings are blackened within a year or two of being put up. Halting at one place I counted the factory chimneys I could see and there were 33. But it was very misty as well as smoky - there would have been many more visible on a clear day. I doubt whether there are any architecturally decent buildings in the town..... At night the hilliness creates fine effects because you look across from one hillside to the other and see the lamps twinkling like stars.

Huge jets of flame shoot periodically out of the roofs of the foundries and show a splendid rosy colour through the smoke and steam. When you get a glimpse inside you see enormous fiery serpents of red hot and white hot iron being rolled out into rails. In the central slummy part of the town are the 'little bosses' i.e. smaller employers who are making chiefly cutlery. I don't think I ever saw in my life so many broken windows. Some of these workshops have hardly a pane of glass in their windows and you would not believe they were inhabitable if you did not see the employees, mostly girls, at work inside."

3 March

he says of his landlord:

"Mixed up with his political feelings is the usual local patriotism of the Yorkshireman and much of his conversation consists of comparison between London and Sheffield to the detriment of the former. Sheffield is held to lead London in everything, e.g. on the one hand the new housing schemes in Sheffield are immensely superior, and on the other hand the Sheffield slums are more squalid than anything can show. ... No one up here seems to have heard of any place in the south of England except London. If you come from the south you are assumed to be a cockney however often you deny it."

Anna Seward
COLEBROOKE DALE

"Warn'd by the Muse, if Birmingham should draw, in future years, from more congenial climes Her massy ore, her labouring sons recall,

And sylvan Colebrook's winding vales restore To beauty and to song, content to draw From unpoetic scenes her rattling stores,Massy and dun; if, thence supplied, she fail, Britain, to glut thy rage commercial, see Grim Wolverhampton lights her smouldering fires, And SHEFFIELD, smoke-involv'd; dim where she stands Circled by lofty mountains, which condense Her dark and spiral wreaths to drizzling rains, Frequent and sullied; as the neighbouring hills Ope their deep veins, and feed her cavern'd flames; While, to her dusky sister, Ketley yields, From her long-desolate, and livid breast, The ponderous metal. No aerial forms On Sheffield's arid moor, or Ketley's heath, E'er wove the floral crowns, or smiling stretch'd The shelly scepter; - there no Poet rov'd to catch bright inspirations.. Blush, ah, blush"

Daniel Defoe
A TOUR THROUGH THE WHOLE ISLAND OF GREAT BRITAIN (1724)

" Leaving Doncaster, we turned out of the road a little way to the left, where we had a fair view of that ancient cutlering town, called Sheffield. The town is very populous and large, the streets narrow and the houses dark and black, occasioned by the continued smoke of the forges, which are always at work."

Bibliography and suggested reading

The Early Years of Cinema in Sheffield
Clifford H Shawe and Stuart R Smith
ISBN 09526036-08
Fascinating tales of the old picture houses, many now knocked down

Dramatic Story of the Sheffield Flood
Peter Machin

Put Yourself in his Place
Charles Reade
A splendid old Victorian novel of grinding, rattening, unions, love and a flood. Inspired by true historical events in Sheffield

Collins Gem Guide to Wild Flowers
Marjorie Blamey and Ricard Fitter
ISBN 0 00 458 801 0
Ideal for sticking in the pocket when wandering wasteland, graveyards etc.

The Illustrated Guide to Sheffield 1879, Pawson and Brailsford
An old guide to the city and surrounding area, complete with lovely old etchings and advertisements

Buffalo Bill's British Wild West
Alan Gallop
ISBN 0 7509 27 02 X
History of William Cody's tour of Edwardian and Victorian Britain between 1887 and 1903

Sheffield Walkabout
Stephen McClarence and
Norah Rodgers   ISBN 086321 0856

Peeks at the Past in Sheffield and the Surrounding Area Vol 1
Ann Beedham ISBN 0 9544045 0 5

Endcliffe Hall in the Manor of Hallamshire
D Hindmarch and A J Podmore

Endcliffe Hall Auction catalogue Maple & Co.

Water Power on the Sheffield Rivers
Edited by David Crossley
ISBN 0 950660 12 4
Extremely detailed look at mills and wheels on the Don, Loxley and Rivelin

A-Z of Sheffield Public Houses
Michael Liversidge ISBN 0 9534267 1 8

The Life and Adventures of Harvey Teasdale, the Converted Clown and Man Monkey'
Harvey Teasdale's Biography can be found in the Local Studies Library

The Collected Essays, Journalism and Letters of George Orwell, Volume 1, An Age Like This
Edited by Sonia Orwell and Ian Angus
ISBN 0 14 00 3151 0

The Road to Wigan Pier George Orwell

Giants of Sheffield Steel
Geoffrey Tweedale

One Great Workshop
The Buildings of the Sheffield Metal Trades
English Heritage
ISBN 1873592 66 3
A well produced small book with photos and diagrams about the places used in steel production

Some Sheffield Organs
CW Andrews
ISBN 1 90 2918 07 X

Mighty Music at the Movies
Fred Turley
ISBN 185048 0087

Beer Matters
Monthly Magazine of The Campaign for Real Ale (Sheffield and District Branch)

Wardsend Whispers
Peter Quincey

Leaven of Life, The Story of George Henry Fletcher
Nellie Connole (1961)

The Memoirs of Ann, Lady Fanshawe